THE AWAKENING OF FAITH

*Prepared for the Columbia College Program
of Translations from the Oriental Classics
Wm. Theodore de Bary, Editor*

THE

AWAKENING OF FAITH

ATTRIBUTED TO
AŚVAGHOSHA

TRANSLATED, WITH COMMENTARY

BY

Yoshito S. Hakeda

COLUMBIA UNIVERSITY PRESS

NEW YORK

Yoshito S. Hakeda is Assistant Professor of Chinese and Japanese at Columbia University

Portions of this work were prepared under a grant from the Carnegie Corporation and a contract with the U. S. Office of Education for the production of texts to be used in undergraduate education. The draft translations so produced have been used in the Columbia College Oriental Humanities program and have subsequently been revised and expanded for publication in the present form.

ISBN 0-231-08336-X *Paperbound*

ISBN: 0-231-03025-8 *Clothbound*

Copyright © 1967 Columbia University Press

Library of Congress Catalog Card Number: 67-13778

Manufactured in the United States of America

Fourth cloth and third paperback printing.

FOREWORD

The *Awakening of Faith* is one of the Translations from the Oriental Classics by which the Committee on Oriental Studies has sought to transmit to Western readers representative works of the major Asian traditions in thought and literature. These are works which in our judgment any educated man should have read. Frequently, however, this reading has been denied him by the lack of suitable translations. All too often he has had to choose between excerpts in popular anthologies on the one hand, and on the other heavily annotated translations intended primarily for the specialist, which in many cases are out of date or out of print. Here we offer translations of whole works, based on scholarly studies, but written for the general reader as well as the specialist.

Of the major traditions of Oriental thought Chinese and Japanese Buddhism is the least well represented by competent translations, despite the quantity of secondary writing on the subject. This is due in part to linguistic difficulties. In the case of the *Awakening of Faith,* one confronts also the inherent subtlety and complexity of its basic ideas. Though these concepts have entered into Mahayana philosophy as a whole and are accepted by the leading schools, this wide currency derives not from their common appeal or ease of access to the Buddhist faithful, but to their profundity in dealing with the central problems of Buddhism. In this sense the *Awakening of Faith* defies popularization. Its very conciseness and apparent simplicity will only confound the reader not well versed in the teachings of Buddhism.

Professor Hakeda has done a great service in providing a straightforward translation with explanatory notes, drawing on his own extensive learning to interpret these pregnant but often enigmatic lines. In the process he has distilled a great mass of earlier commentary in order to convey simply what we must know in order to grasp the essential meaning.

WM. THEODORE DE BARY

PREFACE

The *Awakening of Faith* is one of the basic texts of Mahayana Buddhism, used by most of its major schools. The popularity of the text in East Asian Buddhism is well attested by the numerous works written on it throughout the ages in China, Korea, and Japan. It is hoped that this translation of the work will prove of value to Western readers in increasing their understanding of the basic tenets and practices of Mahayana Buddhism, and that it will assist them to become more familiar with that rich and important branch of the Buddhist religion which, along with the other great religious and philosophical systems of Asia, is rapidly coming to be recognized as part of the cultural heritage of all mankind.

In preparing this translation I have received financial assistance from the Committee on Oriental Studies at Columbia University, for which I would like to express my gratitude. The final portion of the work was supported under a contract in the U.S. Office of Education under which the Committee is preparing texts for foreign area studies. I also wish to acknowledge my indebtedness to Professor Wm. Theodore de Bary, who encouraged me to undertake this project, and who read the manuscript and offered invaluable suggestions; to Professor Burton Watson for reading the manuscript and painstakingly comparing the translation with the original line by line, improving on its style at many points; and to Dr. Philip Yampolsky, Mr. Robert Olson, and Mr. Fred Underwood for their pertinent suggestions. Without their help and encouragement, this work could not have been completed.

YŌSHITO S. HAKEDA

Columbia University
March 1, 1966

CONTENTS

ix

CONTENTS

INTRODUCTION

Introduction

History of the Text

The text known as the *Awakening of Faith in the Mahayana* (*Ta-ch'eng ch'i-hsin lun*) is a short treatise occupying only nine pages in the Taisho edition of the Chinese Tripitaka.[1] The reconstructed Sanskrit title of the work is *Mahāyāna-śraddhotpāda-śāstra;* it is said to have been written in Sanskrit by Aśvaghosha and translated into Chinese in A.D. 550 by the famous Indian translator of Buddhist texts, Paramārtha. No Sanskrit version of the text exists today, however, and all our knowledge of the work is based upon this Chinese version, and a second version that dates from a somewhat later period.

The work is a comprehensive summary of the essentials of Mahayana Buddhism, the product of a mind extraordinarily apt at synthesis. It begins with an examination of the nature of the Absolute or enlightenment and of the phenomenal world or nonenlightenment, and discusses the relationships that exist between them; from there it passes on to the question of how man may transcend his finite state and participate

3

in the life of the infinite while still remaining in the midst of the phenomenal order; it concludes with a discussion of particular practices and techniques that will aid the believer in the awakening and growth of his faith. In spite of its deep concern with philosophical concepts and definitions, therefore, it is essentially a religious work, a map drawn by a man of unshakable faith which will guide the believer to the peak of understanding. But the map and the peak are only provisional symbols, skillful and expedient ways employed to bring men to enlightenment. The text and all the arguments in it exist not for their own sake, but for the sake of this objective alone. The treatise is, indeed, a true classic of Mahayana Buddhism.

The style of the work is extremely terse. It is evident that the author took the utmost pains to make the text as succinct as possible. In fact, the text was designed for his intellectual contemporaries in the fifth or sixth century who, according to the author, "looked upon the wordiness of extensive discourses as troublesome, and who sought after what was comprehensive, terse, and yet contained much meaning." [2] As noted earlier, the author has succeeded in presenting a summary of the principles and basic methods of practice of Mahayana Buddhism in a form terse enough to delight his most exacting contemporaries, and for them the text may not have presented any particular difficulties. But for us today, who are so remote from him in time, the very effort of the author to write concisely is a hindrance to our understanding. As Conze, commenting upon a similar text of Buddhist doctrine, has put it, "We at present must reconstruct laboriously what 1,500 years ago seemed a matter of course." [3] It is indeed as though the author had written in the spirit of the ancient Sanskrit grammarians, who were said to have rejoiced, as over the birth of a son, when they were able to save even a syllable in the formulation of their grammatical

4

rules. This is especially true in the more theoretical sections in the first half of the text, where it is almost impossible to understand certain passages without the aid of commentaries. Other difficulties arise from the nature of the Chinese language which, though highly symbolic and suggestive, lacks the logical precision of Sanskrit. The fact that we have no Sanskrit or Tibetan version of the text to assist our understanding of the Chinese makes the problem of interpretation doubly difficult.

The intrinsic difficulty of the text, as well as the high esteem in which it has been held over the centuries, accounts for the fact that more than 170 commentaries have been written on it.[4] In spite of this mass of exegetical material, however, many problems remain unsolved, while the methods of modern critical scholarship, when applied to the text, have raised new problems concerning the date and authorship of the work. Japanese scholars, joined later by Chinese and European scholars, have since the turn of the century engaged in heated debate over such questions.[5] Some have gone so far as to assert that the text is a forgery, denying the hitherto unquestioned Indian authorship and the assumption that the text represents a Chinese translation of a Sanskrit original; instead, attempts have been made to postulate one or another Chinese Buddhist writer as the true author. No conclusive evidence has so far been brought forth either to support or disprove these theories.

One thing is clear, however, from evidence within the text itself: that it was not written by the Aśvaghosha who lived in the first or second century A.D. and who has been honored as the first Sanskrit poet of the *kāvya* or court poetry style, the earliest dramatic writer in India whose work has survived, and the distinguished predecessor of the great Kālidāsa. Only three works are agreed upon with certainty by Indologists as having been written by this Aśvaghosha, among many other works preserved, mainly in Chinese and Tibetan translations, which bear his name. These are *Buddhacarita* (Life of Buddha);[6] *Saundarananda* (Nanda the Fair);[7] and *Śāriputra-prakaraṇa* (Play on Śāriputra).[8] The first two are classical Sanskrit epics and the last is a drama discovered in Central Asia. No evidence of Mahayana thought can be detected in any of these works; they deal strictly with the doctrines of the Theravada or Hinayana branch of Buddhism. Since the *Awakening of Faith* is dominated by doctrines which did not appear until a few centuries after the time of Aśvaghosha and which are typical of Mahayana thought, it is evident that the work could not have been written by the Aśvaghosha we know. It remains an open question, however, whether the text was produced by some anonymous writer in the fifth or sixth century and was attributed to the great Indian poet, or whether it was written by some other man with the name of Aśvaghosha. Just as there were at least two masters with the name Nāgārjuna, for example, one the founder of the Madhyamika School of Buddhism in the second century A.D., the other a master of later Tantric Buddhism, so it is not surprising that there should be more than one Aśvaghosha. As a matter of fact, one commentary on the *Awakening of Faith* mentions six Buddhist teachers with the name Aśvaghosha.[9] Moreover, we must keep in mind the traditional Indian attitudes toward authorship and the attribution thereof. Not only the discourses in the Pāli canon, which are of fairly early origin, but the sutras of Mahayana Buddhism are represented as the words of the historical Buddha, though many of them date from several hundred years or more after the Buddha's death. Far from representing a spirit of irresponsibility or deceit, such attributions were made in a spirit of sincere piety. Unlike the modern author, who clamors for recognition, the sutra writers of ancient Buddhism deliberately effaced their own identity for the greater glory of their religion. In appraising the work, it seems to be best to set aside the question of authorship and concentrate upon content. Unless some new historical evidence comes to light, we will probably never know who the author of the *Awakening of Faith* actually was.

The fact that Aśvaghosha's name was attached to the text, however, undoubtedly has had much to do with its popularity. He is known in Chinese as Ma-ming or "Horse-neighing," a literal translation of Aśva-ghosha; the name derives from the saying that his poems were so moving that when they were recited even the horses neighed in response. So great is the love and respect that Aśvaghosha commanded as a poet and religious writer that he has been honored with the title of Bodhisattva, and it is easy to imagine why any writer would be happy to bear such a name, or have such a name associated with the text he composed.

Paramārtha, the alleged translator of the text, is equally eminent, the translations credited to his name running to over 300 *chüan* in volume. Paramārtha (499–569) was a monk from Ujjayini in West India who came to China over the southern sea route in 546. According to the *Li-tai san-pao chi*, a catalogue of Buddhist works compiled by Fei Ch'ang-fang in 597, the *Awakening of Faith* was translated by Paramārtha in 550. If this date is accepted—and if Paramārtha did indeed make the translation—we may assume that his knowledge of Chinese was, after only four years of residence in China, hardly sufficient to the task and that he must have relied heavily upon Chinese assistants; in fact, it might be wiser to regard the work as an original composition in Chinese rather than a translation from the Sanskrit.

Whatever the circumstances of its production, the text of the *Awakening of Faith* seems to have spread rapidly and to have been accepted without question as the work of Aśvaghosha. Thus in the earliest extant commentary,[10] that of the monk T'an-yen (516–88), written in all probability between 581 and 587,[11] it is taken for granted that it is the work of Aśvaghosha and that the translation was made by Paramārtha. Eminent Buddhist monks of the sixth and seventh centuries, such as Chi-tsang (549–623), quoted freely from the text, unhesitatingly attributing its authorship to Aśvaghosha. It would appear, therefore, that Chinese readers of the time did not harbor any serious doubts about the authenticity of the text and the translation. Modern scholars are more skeptical. They point to the fact that another early catalogue of Buddhist translations, that compiled by Fa-ching in 594, lists the *Awakening of Faith* in the doubtful section.[12] They find further indication of its dubious nature in the fact that no Tibetan translation of the text exists, that there is no reliable evidence of its having circulated in India, and that certain elements of the text are similar to texts which have been identified as forgeries composed in China.

To make the situation more complicated, there is a second translation of the same text[13] which is known to have been made by a monk named Śikshānanda about 150 years after that of Paramārtha. This monk was a native of Khotan in Central Asia and died in China in 710. One rather doubtful source tells us that Śikshānanda brought the Sanskrit text of the *Awakening of Faith* with him when he came to China, and that he found another old Sanskrit manuscript of the work in China.[14] Another source claims that the Sanskrit text from which Śikshānanda made his translation was in fact a translation into Sanskrit of the earlier Chinese version of the text and had been produced by the famous scholar and translator Hsüan-tsang (602–664).[15] According to proponents of this theory, the existence of such a Sanskrit translation may be explained by a passage in the biography of Hsüan-tsang in the *Hsü kao-seng-chuan* (Further biographies of eminent monks) by Tao-hsüan (596–667), which states that "upon the request of Indian priests, Hsüan-tsang translated the text of the *Awakening of Faith* from Chinese into Sanskrit and circulated it throughout all of India." [16]

Whatever its origin, this later version of the *Awakening of Faith* never enjoyed the same popularity as the earlier version attributed to Paramārtha. This may be seen from the fact that there is only one commentary on it in existence, the work of the famous Ming dynasty monk Chih-hsü (1599–1655). This second version of the text, if it in fact represents a new translation from a Sanskrit original, was obviously done with constant reference to the older version, from which it borrows words, phrases, or whole clauses with little or no modification.[17] Generally speaking, the differences between the two versions are so insignificant that they merit no detailed discussion here. It need only be noted that phrases or passages which are particularly difficult or ambiguous in the older version are often omitted in the later one, or replaced by passages which are more readily understandable. The later version is therefore smoother and easier to read, and may often be used as a kind of commentary on or interpretation of the earlier version, providing simple though often rather superficial solutions to the troublesome passages of the older text.

Among the standard commentaries on the *Awakening of Faith*, that of Hui-yüan (523–92),[18] that written by the Korean monk Wŏnhyo (617–86),[19] and that of Fa-tsang (643–712)[20] have been regarded as the finest. Among these, the last, by Fa-tsang, has been accepted as the final authority for a correct understanding of the text. In Buddhism, not only texts but important commentaries as well have often been treated as the subject of intensive study, and this by Fa-tsang on the *Awakening of Faith* has been much discussed and commented upon. There is another important commentary on the *Awakening of Faith* which deserves notice, for it too has been intensively studied and has inspired the writing of 36 subcommentaries.[21] This is the commentary attributed to a man named Nāgārjuna,[22] about whom nothing is known. Because Kūkai (774–835), the founder of the Shingon School of Buddhism in Japan, made much use of this commentary in his systematization of Shingon doctrine and included it in the requirements for study for his students, it has played a role of particular importance in the history of Shingon Buddhism in Japan up to the present day.

The *Awakening of Faith* has exerted a strong influence upon other schools of Buddhism as well. As we have already noted, Fa-tsang, the third patriarch and the greatest systematizer of the Hua-yen School of Buddhism, wrote what was regarded as the definitive commentary on the *Awakening of Faith,* and moreover used this text as a foundation in creating his systematization of Hua-yen doctrine,[23] and for this reason the text has often been thought of as peculiarly the property of the Hua-yen School. It is not surprising, therefore, that scholars of the Hua-yen School in China, Korea, and Japan have produced many works dealing with the text and with Fa-tsang's interpretation of it. For example, Tsung-mi (780–841), the fifth patriarch of the Hua-yen School, also wrote a commentary on the *Awakening of Faith* and used its doctrines as a foundation in his attempts to synthesize the three religions of China, Confucianism, Taoism, and Buddhism, in his essay entitled *Yüan-jen lun* (Essential nature of man).[24]

The *Awakening of Faith* has also been highly esteemed in the Ch'an or Zen School of Buddhism. Shen-hsiu (d. 706), the leader of the so-called Northern School of Ch'an, made the text an essential part of his course of study,[25] and its influence is clearly discernible in later Ch'an teaching as well. Finally, because one passage in the text (see translation, p. 102) recommends the practice of faith in Amitābha Buddha as an expedient means for the attainment of salvation, the *Awakening of Faith* has been highly esteemed by followers of the Pure Land School, which counsels implicit faith in the saving power of Amitābha. Some scholars have questioned the authenticity of this particular passage, however, and it is not clear what influence, if any, the text has had upon the development of Pure Land doctrine. One authority on Buddhism has even gone so far as to state that the philosophical ideas expressed in the *Awakening of Faith,* along with those of the school of Consciousness-Only (*Wei-shih*) and of Ch'an, played an important part in the development of Neo-Confucian thought in Sung China.[26] If this last assertion is true, then it may be said that the *Awakening of Faith* has had, both directly and indirectly, a truly great influence upon the thought and religion of the Far East.

Content of the Text

The text opens with an invocation and closes with a prayer. What lies between, the main body of the work, is divided into five parts. In Part One, the author gives eight reasons for writing the work. In Part Two, he presents an outline which is to be developed and elaborated upon in the discussions that follow. In Part Three, he takes up the theoretical tenets of Mahayana doctrine listed in the outline; in Part Four, the practical applications of the theories discussed in the preceding section; and in Part Five, the specific types of devotional practice recommended by the author and the benefits to be received therefrom.

The contents of the text have traditionally been summarized as a discourse on "One Mind, Two Aspects, Three Greatnesses, Four Faiths, and Five Practices." This summary does not touch upon all the points mentioned in the work, but it nevertheless serves as a convenient guide to its principal tenets. As such, it has proved useful to those who are giving instruction in the text and has traditionally been recommended to novices for memorization. The summary links up to the parts of the text in the following manner:

Subjects of Discussion	Parts of the Text
(theoretical)	
One Mind	Part Two: Outline
Two Aspects of One Mind	Part Three: Inter-
Three Greatnesses of One Mind	pretation
(practical)	
Four Faiths	Part Four: Faith
Five Practices	Part Four: Practice

Among these five subjects, the most difficult to understand is the first, the concept of One Mind. The following two subjects impose much less difficulty on the reader providing he has correctly understood the first subject, and the last two subjects, dealing as they do with practice rather than theory, present almost no difficulty at all. It may be useful to the reader, therefore, to present here some explanatory remarks upon this key concept of One Mind, and its relationship to the Two Aspects which constitute the second subject.

In the author's system of thought, the all-inclusive Reality, the unconditional Absolute, is called Suchness. When it engages the realms of being, it is expressed in terms of Mind, i.e., One Mind, the Mind of sentient being, the essential nature of Mind, etc. The Mind, therefore, represents the Absolute as it is expressed in the temporal order. The Mind necessarily contains within itself two orders or aspects—the transcendental and the phenomenal, the universal and the particular, the infinite and the finite, the static and the dynamic, the sacred and the profane, the Absolute and the relative, and so forth. The Absolute order, therefore, does not exist apart from the relative order; rather, they differ epistemologically but not ontologically. Man is presented as being located at the intersection of these opposing orders. The state of man, who belongs intrinsically to the Absolute order and yet in actuality remains in the phenomenal, finite, and profane order, is expressed in terms of the *Tathāgata-garbha* or "Matrix of Tathāgata." An understanding of this important term may prove to be the clue to the comprehension of the entire text.

The concept of the "Matrix of Tathāgata" grew up out of attempts to explain how man, while residing in the temporal order, at the same time may possess the potential ability to instate or reinstate himself in the infinite order; that is, in Buddhist terms, to attain enlightenment; or, in more popular terms, to gain salvation. The term *Tathāgata* was originally one of the epithets given to the historical Buddha, Śākyamuni, but it later came to be used in Mahayana Buddhism in a much broader sense. In the compound *Tathāgata-garbha*, it denotes Suchness, the Absolute, or the Eternal Buddha (Dharmakaya). The word *garbha,* meaning a matrix, germ, or embryo, symbolizes the receptacle of *Tathāgata* or the Absolute. It is Suchness in man, the Buddha-nature which is a part of the intrinsic nature of all men, the element of original enlightenment, the potentiality for salvation that waits to be actualized.

This concept of the "Matrix of Tathāgata" had been unknown in the earlier form of Buddhism, the Theravada, often referred to somewhat derogatorily by the Mahayanists as the Hinayana or Lesser Vehicle. Even among the Mahayana thinkers of India it did not develop as an independent system or school of thought in the way that the Madhyamika or Yogacara did, though the concept is explicitly manifested in various Mahayana sutras and other writings, especially in the later Tantric Buddhist texts. It was the Chinese monk Fa-tsang (643–712) who, in his definitive commentary on the *Awakening of Faith,* for the first time drew attention to the great importance of this concept, to which he felt proper notice had hitherto not been paid either in India or China. In the introduction to his commentary to the *Awakening of Faith,*[27] Fa-tsang made an attempt to classify all Indian Buddhism under the following four categories: (1) Hinayana; (2) Madhyamika; (3) Yogacara; and (4) *Tathāgata-garbha.* As the important works belonging to the last, he lists such texts as the *Lankāvatāra Sūtra,*[28] *Ratnagotra-śāstra,*[29] and the *Awakening of Faith,* with a short remark that this doctrine represents the theory of the interpenetration of the universal (*li*) and the particular (*shih*). In the introduction to his publication of the Sanskrit text of the *Ratnagotra-śāstra,* the editor, E. H. Johnston, remarks on the essentials of the text: "The ultimate reality consists of an Absolute, called the *dharmakāya,* but which has several other names to indicate various aspects of it such as *Tathāgata, tathatā, dharmadhātu;* the *sattvadhātu,* the sphere of individual, phenomenal existence, is merely the *dharmadhātu* in its temporal aspect, which is to be found in each being of the *sattvadhātu* in the shape of the *Tathāgata-garbha.* The latter is defined as the *cittaprakriti* [essential nature of Mind], which is *pariśuddha* [pure], that is, not only pure from all time but incapable of defilement, and *prabhāsvara,* 'radiant,' implying presumably that it is spiritual, not material, in essence. . . ."[30] This remark can immediately be applied to the concept of the

"Matrix of Tathāgata" as it is expressed in the *Awakening of Faith*. From the point of view of the history of Buddhist thought, the *Awakening of Faith* may be regarded as representing the highest point in the development of the *Tathāgata-garbha* concept in Mahayana Buddhism.[31]

The basic assumption of the text is the belief in the Absolute which, as we have seen, is at the same time both transcendental and immanent. What is real is Suchness alone; all else is unreal, a mere appearance only, because it is relative, being devoid of independent self-nature or own-being. Metaphysically, the author may be defined as taking the stand of monism; dualism, pluralism, materialism, and nihilism are all alike rejected. However, to define the author's view in such a way would, we must remember, not be acceptable from his own point of view, for, according to his views, to advocate any *ism* at all is merely another type of biased and partial approach which may in fact blind one. The approach of the text is dialectical and iconoclastic, yet in the end essentially religious.

What may be baffling to the reader of the translation is the abundant use of underdefined, sometimes undefined, terms which may be regarded as belonging to the vocabulary of theology, epistemology, psychology, or even biology. The difficulty results basically from the monistic outlook of the text, as well as in part from the author's attitude toward his work. The entire text, in a sense, is an outline which necessarily requires further elucidation and exegesis. The effort of the author to present his outline as succinctly as possible has resulted in insufficient definition of the terms used and underdeveloped argument. Furthermore, the author has made an attempt to systematize all phases of Mahayana teaching and practice under the simplest, most fundamental, yet universal formulas, with the use of various religious, philosophical, and psychological terms that represent many different trends in the Mahayana teaching of his time. The best attitude to take when reading the text is, perhaps, to try to understand the symbolical significance of these terms in their context and the intention of the argument, putting aside as much as possible the more commonly accepted definitions of such terms.

The text, as we have noted, sets out to give a concise and logically ordered summary of Mahayana doctrine. It therefore deliberately eschews most of the literary devices and flourishes which characterize so many of the Mahayana sutras and other texts of Indian Buddhism. There are no anecdotes or dramatic episodes, no poems or descriptive passages. Even the fondness for hyperbole which is such a marked characteristic of the Indian mind figures only in vestigial form in such conventional expressions as "defilements more numerous than the sands of the Ganges." The text accordingly lacks the imaginativeness and rich imagery of the great Mahayana sutras, but it also avoids their repetitiousness and unwieldy proportions. Its virtues are concision, orderliness of presentation, and—within the limitations of its rather obscure terminology—logic of ideas.

To the best of the translator's knowledge, there are three English translations of the *Awakening of Faith*. One was done by Dr. D. T. Suzuki in 1900 from the later Chinese translation attributed to Śikshānanda;[32] the other two were done by the Rev. Timothy Richard in 1907,[33] and by Bhikshu Wai-tao and Dwight Goddard in 1937,[34] both from the older Chinese translation of Paramārtha.

It is in a way unfortunate that Dr. Suzuki's translation was done from the later Chinese text, which has not played a significant role in traditional Buddhism, though Dr. Suzuki lists in his footnotes some of the important disagreements between the new and the old versions of the text. His translation, nevertheless, is the most reliable among the three.

The translation done by the Rev. Timothy Richard suffers from an attempt to read Christianity into the text. Mr. Richard found a striking similarity between the religious thought of the text and that of Christianity. In his introduction he remarks:

If it be, as it is more and more believed, that the Mahayana Faith is not Buddhism, properly so called, but an Asiatic form of the same Gospel of our Lord and Saviour Jesus Christ, in Buddhist nomenclature, differing from the old Buddhism just as the New Testament differs from the Old, then it commands a world-wide interest, for in it we find an adaptation of Christianity to ancient thought in Asia, and the deepest bond of union between the different races of the East and the West, viz., the bond of a common religion. . . . The almost universal reception of the doctrines contained in this book by both the East and the West constitutes to my mind its highest claim to our attention. . . .[35]

Though, as may be judged from these remarks, the translator is extremely sympathetic to the text, his translation inevitably is more Christian than Buddhist in tone.

The translation made by Bhikshu Wai-tao and Dwight Goddard suffers from an excessive freedom in rendition. The translators claim that "the teaching of Ashvaghosha is seen now for the first time in its true colors as a profoundly inspiring psychological appeal designed to awaken faith in the minds of all seekers for Truth." [36] To the present writer, however, it seems that these two translators have done their work rather too freely. To begin with, the translation is incomplete. In addition, it is often difficult to identify the translated passages with the original, and there are many interpolations and unwarranted interpretations. The text being logical rather than aesthetic in nature, this type of translation is hardly satisfactory.

The purpose of the present translation, done from the old

text of Paramārtha, is to present as accurate as possible a translation of the text as it is interpreted in the light of the traditional commentaries, at the same time taking into consideration the results of modern critical scholarship on the text and the history of Buddhist thought in general. An effort has been made to translate the text so as to make it easily accessible to the general reader, but the demands of specialists, who will be comparing it with the original, have also been kept in mind. As a result, the translation is more literal than literary. The translator's main concerns have been philological accuracy and correctness in the interpretation of ideas. He does not flatter himself that he has been successful in all cases, however. A text of such difficulty and conciseness of language may be interpreted in many ways depending upon the translator's *karma*—his predisposition, mentality, life experience, etc. The translation of this type of text, in fact, is not so much a question of technical skill in translating as of the understanding and interpretation of the text. This translation, therefore, is offered as no more than another attempt, to be improved upon by others.

In order to aid the reader in an understanding of the ideas and technical terms of the text, the translator has inserted lines or paragraphs of explanation at appropriate points in the body of the translation, which, it is hoped, will allow the reader to keep abreast of the logical development of the argument and save him the trouble of constantly referring to footnotes. These explanatory comments are set in reduced type. Bracketed words also have been inserted before and after the terse and suggestive passages whenever it was felt that supplementary information was necessary in order to help the reader grasp their meanings. The explanations in the brackets are often based upon the classical commentaries. Material in the footnotes is limited to source references and other information intended mainly for the specialist.

The text used in this translation is that found in the Taisho edition of the Chinese Tripitaka, No. 1666. Among the Chinese commentaries, that written by Fa-tsang (643–712) has been used most frequently because of its intrinsic value and the position of authority which has been accorded it in traditional Buddhist studies. Among modern works on the text, those by Itō Kazuo, Hisamatsu Shin'ichi, Ui Hakuju, and Shih Yin-shun have proved most useful for a basic understanding of the text. A selected bibliography listing these and other important works on the text has been provided at the end of the translation for further reference.

THE AWAKENING OF FAITH

Invocation

I take refuge in [the *Buddha*,] the greatly Compassionate One, the Savior of the world, omnipotent, omnipresent, omniscient, of most excellent deeds in all the ten directions;

And in [the *Dharma*,] the manifestation of his Essence, the Reality, the sea of Suchness, the boundless storehouse of excellencies;

[And in the *Sangha*, whose members] truly devote themselves to the practice,

May all sentient beings be made to discard their doubts, to cast aside their evil attachments, and to give rise to the correct faith in the Mahayana, that the lineage of the Buddhas may not be broken off.

The text opens with an invocation reflecting the traditional pattern universally adopted by all Buddhists throughout the ages, the manifesto of acceptance of and devotion to the Three Treasures (*tri-ratna*)—the *Buddha*, the *Dharma* (the Teaching), and the *Sangha* (Buddhist Community). This expression of the author's resolution is followed by a prayer that the purpose of the writing of this book may be fulfilled.

"Suchness" is a synonym of the Absolute, *chen-ju* in Chinese, *tathatā* or *bhūta-tathatā* in Sanskrit, which may be translated literally as "Real Suchness," "True Suchness," "the state that is really so," etc. For the sake of brevity, and in agreement with more or less established usage, the rendition "Suchness" is adopted here.

The Contents of the Discourse

There is a teaching (dharma) which can awaken in us the root of faith in the Mahayana, and it should therefore be explained. The explanation is divided into five parts. They are (1) the Reasons for Writing; (2) the Outline; (3) the Interpretation; (4) on Faith and Practice; (5) the Encouragement of Practice and the Benefits Thereof.

I

The Reasons for Writing

Someone may ask the reasons why I was led to write this treatise. I reply: there are eight reasons.

The first and the main reason is to cause men to free themselves from all sufferings and to gain the final bliss; it is not that I desire worldly fame, material profit, or respect and honor.

The second reason is that I wish to interpret the fundamental meaning [of the teachings] of the Tathāgata so that men may understand them correctly and not be mistaken about them.

"Tathāgata" in this context is used as one of the epithets of Buddha, the Awakened One, and is usually interpreted as "Thus come," "Thus gone," or by some as "He who has come from the Truth or Absolute."

The third reason is to enable those whose capacity for goodness has attained maturity to keep firm hold upon an unretrogressive faith in the teachings of Mahayana.

The fourth reason is to encourage those whose capacity for goodness is still slight to cultivate the faithful mind.

The fifth reason is to show them expedient means (*upāya*) by which they may wipe away the hindrance of evil karma, guard their minds well, free themselves from stupidity and arrogance, and escape from the net of heresy.

The sixth reason is to reveal to them the practice [of two methods of meditation], cessation [of illusions] and clear observation (*śamatha* and *vipaśyanā;* Ch., *chih-kuan*), so that ordinary men and the followers of Hinayana may cure their minds of error.

The seventh reason is to explain to them the expedient means of single-minded meditation (*smriti*) so that they may be born in the presence of the Buddha and keep their minds fixed in an unretrogressive faith.

The eighth reason is to point out to them the advantages [of studying this treatise] and to encourage them to make an effort [to attain enlightenment]. These are the reasons for which I write this treatise.

Question: What need is there to repeat the explanation of the teaching when it is presented in detail in the sutras?

Answer: Though this teaching is presented in the sutras, the capacity and the deeds of men today are no longer the same, nor are the conditions of their acceptance and comprehension. That is to say, in the days when the Tathāgata was in the world, people were of high aptitude and the Preacher excelled in his form, mind, and deeds, so that once he had preached with his perfect voice, different types of people all equally understood; hence, there was no need for this kind of discourse. But after the passing away of the Tathāgata, there were some who were able by their own power to listen extensively to others and to reach understanding; there were some who by their own power could listen to very little and yet understand much; there were some who, without any mental power of their own, depended upon the extensive discourses of others to obtain understanding; and naturally there were some who looked upon the wordiness of extensive discourses as troublesome, and who sought after what was comprehensive, terse, and yet contained much meaning, and then were able to understand it. Thus, this discourse is designed to embrace, in a general way, the limitless meaning of the vast and profound teaching of the Tathāgata. This discourse, therefore, should be presented.

PART
2

Outline

The reasons for writing have been explained. Next the outline will be given. Generally speaking, Mahayana is to be expounded from two points of view. One is the principle and the other is the significance.

It should be noted that the term "Mahayana" here is not used in the usual sense of the word, that is, Mahayana versus Hinayana. According to the definition given in the discussion immediately following, Mahayana designates Suchness or the Absolute. The title of the text, the *Awakening of Faith in the Mahayana*, should therefore be understood as the "Awakening of Faith in the Absolute," not in Mahayana Buddhism as distinguished from Hinayana Buddhism.

The principle is "the Mind of the sentient being." This Mind includes in itself all states of being of the phenomenal world and the transcendental world. On the basis of this Mind, the meanings of Mahayana may be unfolded. Why? Because the absolute aspect of this Mind represents the essence (*svabhāva*) of Mahayana; and the phenomenal aspect of this Mind indicates the essence, attributes (*lakshana*), and influences (*kriyā*) of Mahayana itself.[1]

The term "Mind" is used neither as the individual mental faculty nor as mind contrasted with matter. It symbolizes the metaphysical principle as defined in the Introduction (see p. 12). When the term "mind" is thought to be used in this particular sense, the first letter will be capitalized. Some of the synonyms for the "Mind of sentient being" are *Tathāgata-garbha,* "the essential nature of Mind," "One Mind," and "the Fountainhead of Mind." Though they differ in nuance and emphasis, these expressions mean the same thing. This introduction of the principle is abrupt, but no doubt it is intended to impress upon the reader the importance of an awareness of the intrinsic value of the human being as being grounded on the Absolute. Though the term "sentient being" is used for the sake of universal significance, it is obvious that it refers to man.

This paragraph gives the outline to be developed in the discussion in Part Three, Chapter One, "Revelation of True Meaning." The term translated as "phenomenal aspect" is literally "primary cause (*hetu*) and conditions (coordinating causes; *pratyaya*) [for a sentient being to remain only] in the order of birth and death (phenomenal order; samsara), and the characteristics (*lakshana*) [of a sentient being in samsara]." This will be discussed in detail later under the two headings: "The Cause and Conditions of Man's Being in Samsara" and "The Characteristics of Beings in Samsara."

At first glance this outline may appear to be lines of ciphers. Be that as it may, the important thing is that here the Mind is discussed from two viewpoints: the absolute and the phenomenal. As for the absolute aspect, only essence (unconditional and self-identical substance or Being) is mentioned; but in the case of the phenomenal aspect, essence, attributes, and influences are listed. That which is common in the two aspects is the essence; the attributes and influences belong only to the phenomenal aspect of the Mind and not to the absolute aspect.

Of the significance [of the adjective *mahā* (great) in the compound, *Mahāyāna*], there are three aspects: (1) the "greatness" of the essence, for all phenomena (dharma) are identical with Suchness and are neither increasing nor decreasing; (2) the "greatness" of the attributes, for the *Tathāgata-garbha* is endowed with numberless excellent qualities; (3) the "greatness" of the influences, for the influences [of Suchness] give rise to the good causes and effects in this and in the other world alike.

"The significance of the adjective *mahā*" will be discussed in detail in Part Three, Chapter One, Section II, under the three categories: "The Greatness of the Essence of Suchness," "The Greatness of the Attributes of Suchness," and "The Greatness of the Influences of Suchness."

Tathāgata-garbha is an immanent aspect of the Absolute (*tathatā*) in the phenomenal order, in contradistinction to the transcendental aspect of it in the Absolute order; in other words, it is the intrinsic Buddha-nature in all sentient beings yet to be actualized. On *Tathāgata-garbha*, cf. Introduction, p. 13.

[The significance of the term *yāna* (vehicle) in the compound, *Mahāyāna*. The term *yāna* is introduced] because all Enlightened Ones (Buddhas) have ridden [on this vehicle], and all Enlightened Ones-to-be (Bodhisattvas), being led by this principle, will reach the stage of Tathāgata.

"The significance of the term *yāna*" will be elaborated upon in terms of theory in Part Three, Chapter Three, "Analysis of the Types of Aspiration for Enlightenment," and in terms of practice in Part Four, "On Faith and Practice."

PART

3

Interpretation

The part on outline has been given; next the part on interpretation [of the principle of Mahayana] will be given. It
consists of three chapters: (1) Revelation of the True Meaning; (2) Correction of Evil Attachments; (3) Analysis of the
Types of Aspiration for Enlightenment.

CHAPTER ONE

Revelation of True Meaning

I. *One Mind and Its Two Aspects*

The revelation of the true meaning [of the principle of
Mahayana can be achieved] by [unfolding the doctrine] that
the principle of One Mind has two aspects. One is the aspect
of Mind in terms of the Absolute (*tathatā;* Suchness), and the
other is the aspect of Mind in terms of phenomena (samsara;
birth and death). Each of these two aspects embraces all
states of existence. Why? Because these two aspects are
mutually inclusive.

31

The most authoritative interpreter, Fa-tsang, defines "One Mind (*eka-citta;* Ch., *i-hsin*)" as the *Tathāgata-garbha*.[2] It should be noted that "one" is used to indicate "absolute" in the sense of "one without any second," not one among many. On One Mind, cf. Introduction, p. 12.

"Because these two aspects are mutually inclusive": Reality is conceived as the intersection of the Absolute order and the phenomenal order; therefore, it contains in itself both the Absolute and the phenomenal order at once. The Absolute order is thought to be transcendental and yet is conceived as not being outside of the phenomenal order. Again the phenomenal order is thought to be temporal and yet is conceived as not being outside of the Absolute order. In other words, they are ontologically identical; they are two aspects of one and the same Reality. Perhaps the most famous and simplest statement of the relationship between the Absolute and the phenomenal order can be found in the sayings of Nāgārjuna (2d century A.D.), e.g., "There is no difference whatsoever between nirvana (Absolute) and samsara (phenomena); there is no difference whatsoever between samsara and nirvana." [3]

A. The Mind in Terms of the Absolute

The Mind in terms of the Absolute is the one World of Reality (*dharmadhātu*) and the essence of all phases of existence in their totality.[4]

Fa-tsang says of the phrase "in their totality": "Because the two aspects of One Mind, i.e., the Absolute aspect and the phenomenal aspect, are not differentiated, but include each other, the words 'in their totality' are used. The one World of Reality is nothing but the world of samsara. At the same time the world of samsara is nothing but the world of the Absolute. In order to indicate these meanings, the Essence which is the same in both aspects is mentioned." [5]

That which is called "the essential nature of the Mind" is unborn and is imperishable. It is only through illusions that all things come to be differentiated. If one is freed from illusions, then to him there will be no appearances (*lakshana*) of objects [regarded as absolutely independent existences]; therefore all things from the beginning transcend all forms of verbalization, description, and conceptualization and are, in the final analysis, undifferentiated, free from alteration, and indestructible. They are only of the One Mind; hence the name Suchness. All explanations by words are provisional and without validity, for they are merely used in accordance with illusions and are incapable [of denoting Suchness]. The term Suchness likewise has no attributes [which can be verbally specified]. The term Suchness is, so to speak, the limit of verbalization wherein a word is used to put an end to words. But the essence of Suchness itself cannot be put an end to, for all things [in their Absolute aspect] are real; nor is there anything which needs to be pointed out as real, for all things are equally in the state of Suchness. It should be understood that all things are incapable of being verbally explained or thought of; hence, the name Suchness.

"Unborn (*an-utpanna*)" is a technical term used in the sense of "beyond time determination." For further discussion on "Unborn," cf. translation, p. 79.

The statement that the Absolute transcends all modes of thought is constantly repeated in the Buddhist scriptures and commentaries. The ideas expressed in the preceding several lines are found in terse presentation in the following passage by Nāgārjuna: "While the object of thought is absent predication ceases; for, just as in the case of nirvana, the essential nature of all things (*dharmatā—dharma-svabhāva*), which is neither born nor perishes, cannot be predicated." [6]

In regard to the sentence, "The term Suchness is, so to speak, the limit of verbalization wherein a word is used to put an end to words," a Korean monk, Wŏnhyo, in his commentary on this text written in the early part of the eighth century says: "It is just as though one stops the voices with a voice." [7] Following this comment by Wŏnhyo, Fa-tsang explains: "It is just like saying 'Be quiet!' If this voice were not there, other voices would not be made to cease." [8]

The term Suchness (*tathatā*) is symbolic. It is an index to that which is transcendental; it is a provisional device of language on the conceptual plane used in an attempt to establish some sort of communication in a realm where all verbal communication fails.

Question: If such is the meaning [of the principle of Mahayana], how is it possible for men to conform themselves to and enter into it?

Answer: If they understand that, concerning all things, though they are spoken of, there is neither that which speaks, nor that which can be spoken of, and though they are thought of, there is neither that which thinks, nor that which can be thought of, then they are said to have conformed to it. And when they are freed from their thoughts, they are said to have entered into it.

Next, Suchness has two aspects if predicated in words. One is that it is truly empty (*śūnya*), for [this aspect] can, in the final sense, reveal what is real. The other is that it is truly nonempty (*a-śūnya*), for its essence itself is endowed with undefiled and excellent qualities.[9]

To paraphrase in more familiar terms, "*śūnya*-approach" may be replaced by "negative approach" which rejects any affirmative identification of the Absolute with any mode of thought; and "*a-śūnya*-approach" by "positive approach" which affirms the Absolute by means of its attributes and influences. The two approaches are regarded in the text as complementary.

1. *Truly Empty*

[Suchness is empty] because from the beginning it has never been related to any defiled states of existence, it is free from all marks of individual distinction of things, and it has nothing to do with thoughts conceived by a deluded mind.

It should be understood that the essential nature of Suchness is neither with marks nor without marks; neither not with marks nor not without marks; nor is it both with and without marks simultaneously; it is neither with a single mark nor with different marks; neither not with a single mark nor not with different marks; nor is it both with a single and with different marks simultaneously.

This effort at negation of any predication of the essential nature of Suchness is typical of Buddhist ways of thought since early times. Beginning with the famous silence of the Buddha on questions such as whether the universe is permanent or impermanent, or whether the universe is limited or unlimited, this attitude has been maintained by Buddhist thinkers. In particular, in a group of sutras known as the *Prajñāpāramitā* or Wisdom Sutras, the oldest stratum of which belongs to the formative stage of Mahayana Buddhism in the 1st or 2d century B.C., the negative approach was ruthlessly emphasized. Nāgārjuna formulated, on the basis of the Wisdom Sutras, the pattern for refuting any false identification of that which is beyond, so that the Absolute remains absolute and is not brought down to the level of the finite. He gives four alternative predications in order to show the absurdity of affirming any of them. The basic alternatives are two: being and nonbeing, i.e., affirmation and negation. Based on these two alternatives, two more predications are possible by affirming or denying both at once: both being and nonbeing, and neither being nor nonbeing. These four alternatives are negated in the beginning of the sentence; further elaborations follow.

In short, since all unenlightened men discriminate with their deluded minds from moment to moment, they are alienated [from Suchness]; hence, the definition "empty"; but once they are free from their deluded minds, they will find that there is nothing to be negated.[10]

2. *Truly Nonempty*

Since it has been made clear that the essence of all things is empty, i.e., devoid of illusions, the true Mind is eternal, permanent, immutable, pure, and self-sufficient; therefore, it is called "nonempty." And also there is no trace of particular marks to be noted in it, as it is the sphere that transcends thoughts and is in harmony with enlightenment alone.

> This is one of the applications of the method of argument known as "affirmation is negation and negation is affirmation." For example, to say that "this is a pen" is to deny that "this is a teacup." To say that "this is not blue" is to affirm that "this is of some color other than blue." To say that "Suchness is empty" is to suggest that Suchness is something which defies any conceptualization; i.e., to say that Suchness is not this, not that, etc., is to say that Suchness is transcendental, empty of concepts. But this negation does not exclude the possibility of Suchness being seen elsewhere or from a different view or order with which one is not accustomed. Hence there is room to present Suchness, if it is done symbolically, as eternal, permanent, immutable, etc. "Emptiness" does not mean "nonexistence" literally; it is usually used in the sense of "empty of or devoid of a distinct, absolute, independent, permanent, individual entity or being as an irreducible component in a pluralistic world," or of "empty of all predications." According to this way of thinking, even "nonbeing" is a "being," as it is contingent upon "being." The term "empty" results from a dialectic consciousness of transcending this dichotomy of "being" and "nonbeing." In order to prevent the danger of interpreting "emptiness" as nonbeing or as an advocation of nihilism, Nāgārjuna says: "Emptiness (śūnyatā), ill conceived, destroys a stupid man, as would a snake when handled improperly, or a spell badly executed." [11]

B. The Mind in Terms of Phenomena

1. *The Storehouse Consciousness*

The Mind as phenomena (samsara) is grounded on the *Tathāgata-garbha*.[12] What is called the Storehouse Consciousness is that in which "neither birth nor death (nirvana)" diffuses harmoniously with "birth and death (samsara)," and yet in which both are neither identical nor different. This Consciousness has two aspects which embrace all states of existence and create all states of existence. They are: (1) the aspect of enlightenment, and (2) the aspect of nonenlightenment.

"The Storehouse Consciousness (ālaya-vijñāna)": According to the Yogacara School of Mahayana Buddhism, the system of perception, mind, ego-consciousness, and subconscious mind is divided into eight categories: the five sense perceptions, vijñāna [mind], mano-vijñāna [ego-consciousness], and ālaya-vijñāna [Storehouse Consciousness]. The relationship that exists between the Storehouse Consciousness and Suchness—whether they are identical or nonidentical—has been a subject of great contention among the sectarian scholars. What is essential here, according to the text, is that the Storehouse Consciousness be defined as the place of intersection of the Absolute order and of the phenomenal order, or enlightenment and nonenlightenment, in man.

a. The Aspect of Enlightenment

(1) *Original Enlightenment* The essence of Mind is free from thoughts. The characteristic of that which is free from thoughts is analogous to that of the sphere of empty space that pervades everywhere. The one [without any second, i.e., the absolute] aspect of the World of Reality (*dharma-dhātu*) is none other than the undifferentiated Dharmakaya, the "Essence-body" of the Tathāgata. [Since the essence of Mind is] grounded on the Dharmakaya, it is to be called the original enlightenment. Why? Because "original enlightenment" indicates [the essence of Mind (*a priori*)] in contradistinction to [the essence of Mind in] the process of actualization of enlightenment; the process of actualization of enlightenment is none other than [the process of integrating] the identity with the original enlightenment.

"The process of actualization of enlightenment," if translated literally, is the "inception of enlightenment." By this expression the author denotes the entire process from the inception of enlightenment or awakening to the full realization of enlightenment.

(2) *The Process of Actualization of Enlightenment*
Grounded on the original enlightenment is nonenlightenment. And because of nonenlightenment, the process of actualization of enlightenment can be spoken of.

> Original enlightenment is intrinsic, but nonenlightenment is
> accidental. The latter is the unactualized state of the same orig-
> inal enlightenment. That is to say, man is originally enlightened
> or saved, but suffers because he does not realize that he is en-
> lightened or saved and continues on as a blind or faithless man,
> groping for enlightenment or salvation elsewhere. The premise
> is that if man is not enlightened or saved originally, there is no
> possibility of his attaining enlightenment or salvation at all.

Now, to be [fully] enlightened to the fountainhead of
Mind is called the final enlightenment; and not to be enlightened to the fountainhead of Mind, nonfinal enlightenment.

What is the meaning of this? An ordinary man becomes
aware that his former thoughts were wrong; then he is able
to stop (*nirodha*) such thoughts from arising again. Although
this sometimes may also be called enlightenment, [properly
it is not enlightenment at all] because it is not enlightenment
[that reaches the fountainhead of Mind].

The followers of Hinayana, who have some insight, and
those Bodhisattvas who have just been initiated become aware
of the changing state (*anyathātva*) of thoughts and are free
from thoughts which subject to change [such as the existence of a permanent self (atman), etc.]. Since they have
forsaken the rudimentary attachments derived from unwarranted speculation (*vikalpa*), [their experience] is called
enlightenment in appearance.

Bodhisattvas [who have come to the realization] of Dharmakaya become aware of the [temporarily] abiding state (*sthiti*)
of thoughts and are not arrested by them. Since they are free

from their rudimentary [false] thoughts derived from the speculation [that the components of the world are real, their experience] is called approximate enlightenment.

Those Bodhisattvas who have completed the stages of a Bodhisattva and who have fulfilled the expedient means [needed to bring forth the original enlightenment to the fullest extent] will experience the oneness [with Suchness] in an instant; they will become aware of how the inceptions of [the deluded thoughts of] the mind arise (*jāti*), and will be free from the rise of any [deluded] thought. Since they are far away even from subtle [deluded] thoughts, they are able to have an insight into the original nature of Mind. [The realization] that Mind is eternal is called the final enlightenment. It is, therefore, said in a sutra that if there is a man who is able to perceive that which is beyond thoughts he is advancing toward the Buddha wisdom.

Here the author applies, in the analysis of the process of the actualization of enlightenment, the four characteristic states of existence, in reverse order. The four characteristic states (*avasthā*) are: (1) arising—the coming into existence analogous to the birth of a child (*jāti*); (2) abiding—the state of continuity in growth analogous to the stage from childhood to manhood (*sthiti*); (3) change—the stage of changing periods analogous to the period from the prime of life to old age (*anyathātva*); and (4) stopping —the period of senility and destruction (*nirodha*). These four characteristic states, when used in a cosmic sense, designate one cycle of cosmic age that continues with infinite repetition. This application of the four characteristic states of existence in reverse order for the description of the process of the actualization of enlightenment seems to be unknown elsewhere.

The simile of a dream, or of mistaking a rope for a snake, treasured especially in the writings of the Yogacara School of Buddhism, might be helpful in understanding the first sentence of the last paragraph, which is insufficiently explained. To illustrate, only when awake can one realize the true nature of a dream; while dreaming one is not aware that one is dreaming.

Being aware that it was a dream, one can be free from the dream. Similarly, only when a correct view is established can one realize that one's former views were wrong and be able to understand why wrong views were entertained on certain partial or incorrect assumptions. Only then will one be free from the rise of any deluded thoughts.

Though it is said that there is [an inception of] the rising of [deluded] thoughts in the mind, there is no inception as such that can be known [as being independent of the essence of Mind]. And yet to say that the inception [of the rising of deluded thoughts] is known means that it is known as [existing on the ground of] that which is beyond thoughts [i.e., the essence of Mind]. Accordingly, all ordinary people are said not to be enlightened because they have had a continuous stream of [deluded] thoughts and have never been freed from their thoughts; therefore, they are said to be in a beginningless ignorance. If a man gains [insight into] that which is free from thoughts, then he knows how those [thoughts] which characterize the mind [i.e., deluded thoughts] arise, abide, change, and cease to be, for he is identical with that which is free from thoughts. But, in reality, no difference exists in the process of the actualization of enlightenment, because the four states [of rising, abiding, etc.] exist simultaneously and each of them is not self-existent; they are originally of one and the same enlightenment [in that they are taking place on the ground of original enlightenment, as its phenomenal aspects].

And, again, original enlightenment, when analyzed in relation to the defiled state [in the phenomenal order], presents itself as having two attributes. One is the "Purity of Wisdom" and the other is the "Suprarational Functions."

Purity of wisdom and the suprarational functions of the Absolute, or enlightenment, can be discussed only in relation to phenomena, or nonenlightenment. About the Absolute, or enlightenment, in its totally transcendental aspect, nothing can be said.

(a) Purity of Wisdom. By virtue of the permeation (*vāsanā*, perfuming) of the influence of dharma [i.e., the essence of Mind or original enlightenment], a man comes to truly discipline himself and fulfills all expedient means [of unfolding enlightenment]; as a result, he breaks through the compound consciousness [i.e., the Storehouse Consciousness that contains both enlightenment and nonenlightenment], puts an end to the manifestation of the stream of [deluded] mind, and manifests the Dharmakaya [i.e., the essence of Mind], for his wisdom (*prajñā*) becomes genuine and pure.

What is the meaning of this? All modes (*lakshana*) of mind and consciousness [under the state of nonenlightenment] are [the products of] ignorance. Ignorance does not exist apart from enlightenment; therefore, it cannot be destroyed [because one cannot destroy something which does not really exist], and yet it cannot not be destroyed [in so far as it remains]. This is like the relationship that exists between the water of the ocean [i.e., enlightenment] and its waves [i.e., modes of mind] stirred by the wind [i.e., ignorance]. Water and wind are inseparable; but water is not mobile by nature, and if the wind stops the movement ceases. But the wet nature remains undestroyed. Likewise, man's Mind, pure in its own nature, is stirred by the wind of ignorance. Both Mind and ignorance have no particular forms of their own and they are inseparable. Yet Mind is not mobile by nature, and if ignorance ceases, then the continuity [of deluded activities] ceases. But the essential nature of wisdom [i.e., the essence of Mind, like the wet nature of the water] remains undestroyed.

(b) Suprarational Functions. [He who has fully uncovered the original enlightenment] is capable of creating all manner of excellent conditions because his wisdom is pure. The manifestation of his numberless excellent qualities is incessant; accommodating himself to the capacity of other men he responds spontaneously, reveals himself in manifold ways, and benefits them.

(3) *The Characteristics of the Essence of Enlightenment*
The characteristics of the essence of enlightenment have four great significances that are identical with those of empty space or that are analogous to those of a bright mirror.

First, [the essence of enlightenment is like] a mirror which is really empty [of images]. It is free from all marks of objects of the mind and it has nothing to reveal in itself, for it does not reflect any images.

From the Absolute point of view, the plurality of particulars does not exist. What exists is the Absolute only, just as space is one without any second. Division of space is man-made, the result of thought construction made for the sake of convenience; intrinsically it is nonexistent.

Second, [it is, as it were] a mirror, influencing (*vāsanā*) [all men to advance toward enlightenment], serving as the primary cause [of their attaining enlightenment]. That is to say, it is truly nonempty; appearing in it are all the objects of the world which neither go out nor come in; which are neither lost nor destroyed. It is eternally abiding One Mind. [All things appear in it] because all things are real. And none of the defiled things are able to defile it, for the essence of wisdom [i.e., original enlightenment] is unaffected [by defilements], being furnished with an unsoiled quality and influencing all men [to advance toward enlightenment].

Third, [it is like] a mirror which is free from [defiled] objects [reflected in it]. This can be said because the nonempty state [of original enlightenment] is genuine, pure, and bright, being free from hindrances both affectional and intellectual, and transcending characteristics of that which is compounded [i.e., the Storehouse Consciousness].

Fourth, [it is like] a mirror influencing [a man to cultivate his capacity for goodness], serving as a coordinating cause [to encourage him in his endeavors]. Because [the essence of enlightenment] is free from [defiled] objects, it universally illumines the mind of man and induces him to cultivate his capacity for goodness, presenting itself in accordance with his desires [as a mirror presents his appearance].

Of the four arguments, the first and second correspond to the arguments on the two aspects of the Absolute in terms of empty and nonempty. The third and fourth arguments correspond to "Purity of Wisdom" and "Suprarational Functions" in the preceding section.

b. The Aspect of Nonenlightenment

Because of not truly realizing oneness with Suchness, there emerges an unenlightened mind and, consequently, its thoughts. These thoughts do not have any validity to be substantiated; therefore, they are not independent of the original enlightenment. It is like the case of a man who has lost his way: he is confused because of [his wrong sense of] direction. If he is freed from [the notion of] direction altogether, then there will be no such thing as going astray. It is the same with men: because of [the notion of] enlightenment, they are confused. But if they are freed from [the fixed notion of] enlightenment, then there will be no such thing as nonenlightenment. Because [there are men] of unenlightened, deluded mind, for them we speak of true enlightenment, knowing well what this [relative] term stands for. Independent of the unenlightened mind, there are no independent marks of true enlightenment itself that can be discussed.

"Not truly realizing oneness with Suchness": Literally: "Not knowing that the dharma of Suchness is one," or perhaps, "Not knowing that Suchness and dharma (phenomena) are one." In any case, the meaning remains the same. This has been called the "basic ignorance."

The discussion is on the two seemingly opposing concepts of enlightenment and nonenlightenment. From the author's point of view, these polar concepts are not mutually exclusive or contradictory; they are merely relative, since enlightenment is inconceivable in the absence of nonenlightenment; they coexist temporarily, as it were, in mutual dependency, on the ground of the original enlightenment or the Absolute. Neither enlightenment nor nonenlightenment should be considered to be an absolute state. The irrelevancy of taking either of them to be a concrete state of being—in other words, the absurdity of regarding a relative as an Absolute, or a conventional and symbolic expression as literally true—is here demonstrated.

Because of its nonenlightened state, [the deluded mind] produces three aspects which are bound to nonenlightenment and are inseparable from it.

First is the activity of ignorance. The agitation of mind because of its nonenlightened state is called activity. When enlightened, it is unagitated. When it is agitated, anxiety (duḥkha) follows, for the result [i.e., anxiety] is not independent of the cause [i.e., the agitation contingent upon ignorance].

Second is the perceiving subject. Because of the agitation [that breaks the original unity with Suchness], there appears the perceiving subject. When unagitated, [the mind] is free from perceiving.

Third is the world of objects. Because of the perceiving subject, the world of objects erroneously appears. Apart from the perceiving, there will be no world of objects.

Conditioned by the [incorrectly conceived] world of objects, [the deluded mind] produces six aspects.

First is the aspect of the [discriminating] intellect. Depending on the [erroneously conceived] world of objects, the mind develops the discrimination between liking and disliking.

44

Second is the aspect of continuity. By virtue of [the discriminating function of] the intellect, the mind produces an awareness of pleasure and pain [with regard to things] in the world of objects. The mind, developing [deluded] thoughts and being bound to them, will continue uninterrupted.

Third is the aspect of attachment. Because of the continuity [of deluded thoughts], the mind, superimposing its deluded thoughts on the world of objects and holding fast to [the discriminations of liking and disliking] develops attachments [to what it likes].

Fourth is the aspect of the speculation (*vikalpa*) on names and letters [i.e., concepts]. On the basis of erroneous attachments, [the deluded mind] analyzes words which are provisional [and therefore devoid of validity].

Fifth is the aspect of giving rise to [evil] karma. Relying on names and letters [i.e., concepts which have no validity, the deluded mind] investigates names and words and becomes attached to them, and creates manifold types of evil karma.

Sixth is the aspect of anxiety attached to the [effects of evil] karma. Because of the [law of] karma, the deluded mind suffers the effects and will not be free.

It should be understood that ignorance is able to produce all types of defiled states; all defiled states are aspects of nonenlightenment.

c. The Relationships between Enlightenment and Nonenlightenment

Two relationships exist between the enlightened and nonenlightened states. They are "identity" and "nonidentity."

(1) *Identity* Just as pieces of various kinds of pottery are of the same nature in that they are made of clay, so the various magic-like manifestations (*māyā*) of both enlightenment (*anāsrava:* nondefilement) and nonenlightenment

(*avidyā*) are aspects of the same essence, Suchness. For this reason, it is said in a sutra that "all sentient beings intrinsically abide in eternity and are entered into nirvana. The state of enlightenment is not something that is to be acquired by practice or to be created. In the end, it is unobtainable [for it is given from the beginning]." [13] Also it has no corporeal aspect that can be perceived as such. Any corporeal aspects [such as the marks of the Buddha] that are visible are magic-like products [of Suchness manifested] in accordance with [the mentality of men in] defilement. It is not, however, that these corporeal aspects [which result from the suprarational functions] of wisdom are of the nature of nonemptiness [i.e., substantial]; for wisdom has no aspects that can be perceived.

(2) *Nonidentity* Just as various pieces of pottery differ from each other, so differences exist between the state of enlightenment and that of nonenlightenment, and between the magic-like manifestations [of Suchness manifested] in accordance with [the mentality of men in] defilement, and those [of men of ignorance] who are defiled [i.e., blinded] as to the essential nature [of Suchness].

2. *The Cause and Conditions of Man's Being in Samsara*

A literal translation of this title is: "The cause and conditions of birth and death." The cause stands for the aspect of non-enlightenment in the Storehouse Consciousness, i.e., ignorance; the conditions stand for mind and consciousness in the state of nonenlightenment. In short, this section undertakes to deal with the mentality of a man who is unaware of the Absolute order, despite the fact that he is intrinsically in it. In the following argument some similarity can be found between the author's thought and the doctrines of the Yogacara School of Mahayana Buddhism. The Yogacara School advocates the concept of "mind only" and its doctrine is known as subjective idealism. The author presents the subject in his own way, developing the concept of *Tathāgata-garbha,* but some basic ideas and terms must have been taken into his system from Yogacara sources.

That a man is in samsara results from the fact that his mind (*manas*) and consciousness (*vijñāna*) develop on the ground of the Storehouse Consciousness (*citta*). This means that because of [the aspect of nonenlightenment of] the Storehouse Consciousness, he is said to be in possession of ignorance [and thus is bound to remain in samsara].

Citta, manas, and *vijñāna* are synonymous in the earliest phase of Buddhism, indicating "mind" in the ordinary sense of the word. Along with the systematization of and speculation on the Buddha's doctrines, Buddhist thinkers (Abhidharma philosophers) differentiated among them, ascribing unique psychometaphysical meanings to each. The Yogacara School of Buddhism, in an attempt to analyze the levels of mind of the nonenlightened man, established a distinctive use of these terms. According to this School, *citta* corresponds to *ālaya-vijñāna* (Storehouse Consciousness), *manas* to *mano-vijñāna* (ego-conscious mind), and *vijñāna* remains as it was, denoting the ordinary mind and sometimes the five perceptions. Though the author (or translator) uses these same terms, their content is often quite different from that found in Yogacara philosophy. This section, therefore, should be interpreted in the light of the over-all thought of the text, without reference to the Yogacara interpretation of these technical terms. Attempts to equate or harmonize it with Yogacara thought will invite unnecessary confusion and misunderstanding.

a. Mind

[The mentality] which emerges in the state of nonenlightenment, which [incorrectly] perceives and reproduces [the world of objects] and, conceiving that the [reproduced] world of objects is real, continues to develop [deluded] thoughts, is what we define as mind.

This mind has five different names.

The first is called the "activating mind," for, without being aware of it, it breaks the equilibrium of mind by the force of ignorance.

The second is called the "evolving mind," for it emerges contingent upon the agitated mind as [the subject] that perceives [incorrectly].

The third is called the "reproducing mind," [14] for it reproduces the entire world of objects as a bright mirror reproduces all material images. When confronted with the objects of the five senses, it reproduces them at once. It arises spontaneously at all times and exists forever [reproducing the world of objects] in front [of the subject].

The fourth is called the "analytical mind," for it differentiates what is defiled and what is undefiled.

The fifth is called the "continuing mind," for it is united with [deluded] thoughts and continues uninterrupted. It retains the entire karma, good and bad, accumulated in the immeasurable lives of the past, and does not permit any loss. It is also capable of bringing the results of the pain, pleasure, etc., of the present and the future to maturity; in doing so, it makes no mistakes. It can cause one to recollect suddenly the things of the present and the past and to have sudden and unexpected fantasies of the things to come.

The triple world, therefore, is unreal and is of mind only. Apart from it there are no objects of the five senses and of the mind. What does this mean? Since all things are, without exception, developed from the mind and produced under the condition of deluded thoughts, all differentiations are no other than the differentiations of one's mind itself. [Yet] the mind cannot perceive the mind itself; the mind has no marks of its own [that can be ascertained as a substantial entity as such]. It should be understood that [the conception of] the entire world of objects can be held only on the basis of man's deluded mind of ignorance. All things, therefore, are just like the images in a mirror which are devoid of any objectivity that one can get hold of; they are of the mind only and are unreal. When the [deluded] mind comes into being, then various conceptions (dharma) come to be; and when the [deluded] mind ceases to be, then these various conceptions cease to be.

"The triple world, therefore, is unreal and is of mind only": The oldest recorded expression of this statement, encountered in many scriptures of later origin, is found in one of the earliest Mahayana sutras of the 1st or 2d century A.D., called the Ten Stages (Daśabhūmika Sūtra), which was later incorporated, most likely in Central Asia or China, into the Avatamsaka (Hua-yen) Sūtra. This statement was not only taken up by the Hua-yen School, but was also utilized as one of the authentic proofs to provide a foundation to the Yogacara system. In fact, the virtual founder of the Yogacara School, Vasubandhu, composed a commentary on the Daśabhūmika Sūtra.[15] As it appears in the sutra, the original sentence may be translated: "What belongs to this triple world is mind only." [16] The triple world is the world of desire, the world of form or material, and the world of formlessness.

b. Consciousness

What is called "consciousness (vijñāna)" is the "continuing mind." Because of their deep-rooted attachment, ordinary men imagine that I and Mine are real and cling to them in their illusions. As soon as objects are presented, this consciousness rests on them and discriminates the objects of the five senses and of the mind. This is called "vijñāna [i.e., the differentiating consciousness]" or the "separating consciousness." Or, again, it is called the "object-discriminating consciousness." [The propensity for discrimination of] this consciousness will be intensified by both [the intellectual] defilement of holding fast to perverse views and [the affectional] defilement of indulgence in passion.

That the [deluded mind and] consciousness arise from the permeation of ignorance is something that ordinary men cannot understand. The followers of the Hinayana, with their wisdom, likewise fail to realize this. Those Bodhisattvas who, having advanced from their first stage of correct faith by setting the mind [upon enlightenment] through practicing contemplation, have come to realize the Dharmakaya, can partially comprehend this. Yet even those who have reached the final stage of Bodhisattvahood cannot fully comprehend this; only the Enlightened Ones have thorough comprehension of it. Why? The Mind, though pure in its self nature from the beginning, is accompanied by ignorance. Being defiled by ignorance, a defiled [state of] Mind comes into being. But, though defiled, the Mind itself is eternal and immutable. Only the Enlightened Ones are able to understand what this means.

What is called the essential nature of Mind is always beyond thoughts. It is, therefore, defined as "immutable." When the one World of Reality is yet to be realized, the Mind [is mutable and] is not in perfect unity [with Suchness]. Suddenly, [a deluded] thought arises; [this state] is called ignorance.

"Suddenly" is a literal translation of the Chinese adverbial compound *hu-jan*. Here, casually and in a sentence of a few words, the origin of ignorance (*avidyā*) is explained. Ignorance is the most fundamental problem of Buddhism, comparable in its significance to that of original sin in Christianity. The author's avowed determination to make his discourse as brief as possible should be appreciated, but often he has achieved his aim at the risk of being understood incorrectly, or of not being understood at all.

There has been much discussion on the meaning of *hu-jan* in connection with the origin of ignorance, mainly on the basis of interpretations proposed by Fa-tsang, the most celebrated commentator on the text. Following the comment made by a Korean monk named Wŏnhyo,[17] Fa-tsang says of it (1) that ignorance alone becomes the source of defiled states of being. It is the subtlest; no other state of being can be the origin of this. It is therefore said in the text that ignorance emerges suddenly. (2)

Commenting on a quotation from a sutra, he says "suddenly" means "beginninglessly," since the passage quoted makes clear that there is no other state of being prior to the state of ignorance. (3) The word "suddenly" is not used from the standpoint of time, but is used to account for the emergence of ignorance without any instance of·inception.[18] It is clear, then, that Fa-tsang interpreted "suddenly" as "without beginning." Accordingly, the conclusion may be drawn that ignorance, the primary cause of the nonenlightened state of man, has no beginning, but does have an ending, since it disappears with enlightenment.

A monk of Ming China, named Chen-chieh, in his commentary to the *Awakening of Faith* written in 1599, glosses "suddenly" as *pu-chüeh,* which may mean "unconsciously" or "without being aware of the reason." [19]

If *hu-jan* is a translation of a Sanskrit word, the original word *akasmāt* may be posited.[20] *Akasmāt* means "without reason" or "accidentally." If this is correct, the following metaphor quoted by another Chinese monk, Tzu-hsüan (d. 1038) of the Hua-yen School, in interpreting "suddenly" is peculiarly relevant. He writes: "[Ignorance is] like dust which has suddenly collected on a mirror, or like clouds which have suddenly appeared in the sky." [21]

In the earlier part of the text, the claim was made that man is originally enlightened and that ignorance or nonenlightenment are not intrinsic but accidental. Ignorance results from an unconscious and accidental estrangement from the essence of Mind (Suchness). In the absence of the awareness of estrangement, however, the origin of ignorance cannot be an object of intellectual analysis. For the intellect, the origin of ignorance is unimaginable, unless mythologized; hence, "suddenly" would appear to be an excellent solution.

c. Defiled States of Mind

Six kinds of defiled states of mind [conditioned by ignorance] can be identified.

The first is the defilement united with attachment [to atman], from which those who have attained liberation in Hinayana and those [Bodhisattvas] at the "stage of establishment of faith" are free.

The second is the defilement united with the "continuing

mind," from which those who are at the "stage of establishment of faith" and who are practicing expedient means [to
attain enlightenment] can gradually free themselves and free
themselves completely at the "stage of pure-heartedness."

The third is the defilement united with the discriminating
"analytical mind," from which those at the "stage of observ-
ing precepts" begin to be liberated and finally are liberated
completely when they arrive at the "stage of expedient means
without any trace."

The fourth is the [subtle] defilement disunited from the
represented world of objects, from which those at the "stage
of freedom from world of objects" can be freed.

The fifth is the [subtler] defilement disunited from the
"[evolving] mind that perceives" [i.e., the defilement existing
prior to the act of perceiving], from which those at the "stage
of freedom from [evolving] mind" are freed.

The sixth [and most subtle] is the defilement disunited
from the basic "activating mind," from which those Bodhisattvas who have passed the final stage and have gone into the
"stage of Tathāgatahood" are freed.

> "Basic 'activating mind'" means man's propensity to prefer to
> remain in the state of ignorance. It exists prior to the separation
> of the subject and object relationship in the context of non-
> enlightenment. It may be regarded as analogous to the tendency
> toward evil that exists prior to the motivation and commitment
> of evil acts that cause evil karma; it is the basic blindness
> (avidyā), lurking in the deepest level of the subconscious mind.

d. Comments on the Terms Used in the
   Foregoing Discussion

On [the expression] "the one World of Reality is yet to be
realized." From this state those [Bodhisattvas] who have advanced from the "stage of the establishment of faith" to the

"stage of pure-heartedness," after having completed and severed [their deluded thoughts], will be more and more liberated as they advance, and when they reach the "stage of Tathāgatahood," they will be completely liberated.

On "united." By the word "united" [appearing in the first three defilements] is meant that though difference [i.e., duality] exists between the mind (subject) and the datum of the mind (object), there is a simultaneous relation between them in that when the subject is defiled the object is also defiled, and when the subject is purified the object is also purified.

On "disunited." By the word "disunited" is meant that [the second three subtle and fundamental defilements are the aspects of] nonenlightenment on the part of the mind existing prior to the differentiation [into the subject and object relationship]; therefore, a simultaneous relation between the subject and object is not as yet established.

On the "defiled state of mind." It is called "the hindrance originating from defilements," for it obstructs any fundamental insight into Suchness.

On "ignorance." Ignorance is called the "hindrance originating from misconceptions of objects," for it obstructs the wisdom that functions spontaneously in the world.

Because of the defiled [state of] mind, there emerges the subject that perceives [incorrectly; i.e., the evolving mind] and that which reproduces [the reproducing mind] and thus one erroneously predicates the world of objects and causes oneself to deviate from the undifferentiated state [of Suchness]. Though all things are always in quiescence and devoid of any marks of rising, because of the nonenlightenment due to ignorance, one erroneously strays from the dharma [i.e., Suchness]; thus one fails to obtain the wisdom that functions spontaneously by adapting oneself to all circumstances in the world.

"The wisdom that functions spontaneously in the world." Technically this wisdom is called the "later-obtained wisdom" (*pṛṣṭha-labdha-jñāna;* Ch., *hou-tê-chih*). It is the wisdom that, after achieving enlightenment and witnessing the pitiful state of existence of the world, naturally emerges to help save the world. When a man caught in a vicious cycle of frustration awakens to his essential being, returns to the Absolute order, and reinstates Suchness in himself, he can for the first time see the suffering world in its full scope. As eyes cannot see eyes, so as long as he is in the midst of suffering, without transcending it, he cannot see the real state of existence of the world. A keen awareness of the fact that, so long as a man is not awakened, everything is suffering, came to the Buddha after he had attained enlightenment. The well-known words of the Buddha that "everything is suffering (*sarvaṃ duḥkam*)" were, in fact, uttered after he had attained enlightenment. Hence, he was compelled to work for the salvation of the world.

3. *The Characteristics of Beings in Samsara*

In analyzing the characteristics of beings in samsara, two categories may be distinguished. The one is "crude," for [those who belong to this category are] united with the [crude activities of the defiled] mind; the other is "subtle," for [those who belong to this category are] disunited from the [subtle activities of the defiled] mind. [Again, each category may in turn be subdivided into the cruder and the subtler]. The cruder of the crude belongs to the range of mental activity of ordinary men; the subtler of the crude and the cruder of the subtle belong to that of Bodhisattvas; and the subtler of the subtle belongs to that of Buddhas.

Reference is to be made to the "Defiled States of Mind" in the foregoing discussion. The "crude" corresponds to the first three defilements of mind and the "subtle" to the second three defilements of mind.

"The subtler of the subtle [belongs] to that of Buddhas." Does this mean that the Buddhas, the Enlightened Ones, still have some sort of basic defilement, even though it is the subtlest of all? This question was answered by Wŏnhyo,[22] whose words were adapted by Fa-tsang in the following way: "[The range of mental activity belonging to the subtler of the subtle takes place] where there is no separation of subject and object. Since the characteristic of its activity is extremely subtle, only Buddhas can know about it." In the later translation of the text by Śikshānanda this clause is omitted.

These two categories of beings in the phenomenal order come about because of the permeation of ignorance; that is to say, they come about because of the primary cause and the coordinating causes. By the primary cause, "nonenlightenment" is meant; and by the coordinating causes, "the erroneously represented world of objects."

When the primary cause ceases to be, then the coordinating causes will cease to be. Because of the cessation of the primary cause, the mind disunited [from the represented world of objects, etc.] will cease to be; and because of the cessation of the coordinating causes, the mind united [with the attachment to atman, etc.] will cease to be.

Question: If the mind ceases to be, what will become of its continuity? If there is continuity of mind, how can you explain its final cessation?

Answer: What we speak of as "cessation" is the cessation of the marks of [the deluded] mind only and not the cessation of its essence. It is like the case of the wind which, following the surface of the water, leaves the marks of its movement. If the water should cease to be, then the marks of the wind would be nullified and the wind would have no support [on which to display its movement]. But since the water does not cease to be, the marks of the wind may continue. Because only the wind ceases, the marks of its movement cease accordingly. This is not the cessation of water. So it is with ignorance; on the ground of the essence of Mind there is movement. If the essence of Mind were to cease, then people would be nullified and they would have no support. But since the essence does not cease to be, the mind may continue. Because only stupidity ceases to be, the marks of the [stupidity of the] mind cease accordingly. It is not that the wisdom [i.e., the essence] of Mind ceases.

This simile, well known for its occurrence in this text, has been popular among the Buddhist thinkers in the Far East as one of the best means to explain the relationship that exists between phenomena and the Absolute.[24]

Because of the four kinds of permeation, the defiled states and the pure state emerge and continue uninterrupted. They are (1) the pure state, which is called Suchness; (2) the cause of all defilements, which is called ignorance; (3) the deluded mind, which is called "activating mind"; (4) the erroneously conceived external world, which is called the "objects of the five senses and of mind."

The meaning of permeation. Clothes in the world certainly have no scent in themselves, but if man permeates them with perfumes, then they come to have a scent. It is just the same with the case we are speaking of. The pure state of Suchness certainly has no defilement, but if it is permeated by ignorance, then the marks of defilement appear on it. The defiled state of ignorance is indeed devoid of any purifying force, but if it is permeated by Suchness, then it will come to have a purifying influence.

a. Permeation of Ignorance

How does the permeation [of ignorance] give rise to the defiled state and continue uninterrupted? It may be said that, on the ground of Suchness [i.e., the original enlightenment], ignorance [i.e., nonenlightenment] appears. Ignorance, the primary cause of the defiled state, permeates into Suchness. Because of this permeation a deluded mind results. Because of the deluded mind, [deluded thoughts further] permeate into ignorance. While the principle of Suchness is yet to be realized, [the deluded mind], developing thoughts [fashioned in the state] of nonenlightenment, predicates erroneously conceived objects of the senses and the mind. These erroneously conceived objects of the senses and the mind, the coordinating causes in [bringing about] the defiled state, permeate into the deluded mind and cause the deluded mind to attach itself to its thoughts, to create various [evil] karma, and to undergo all kinds of physical and mental suffering.

The permeation of the erroneously conceived objects of the senses and the mind is of two kinds. One is the permeation which accelerates [deluded] thoughts, and the other is the permeation which accelerates attachments.

The permeation of the deluded mind is of two kinds. One is the basic permeation by the "activating mind," which causes Arhats, Pratyeka-buddhas, and all Bodhisattvas to undergo the suffering of samsara, and the other is the permeation which accelerates [the activities of] the "object-discriminating consciousness" and which makes ordinary men suffer from the bondage of their karma.

The word "Arhat" was originally an epithet for the Buddha meaning "worthy," but it came to be used often in Mahayana writings in a derogatory sense to designate the perfected one in Hinayana Buddhism who needs to be retrained in Mahayana Buddhism in order to attain true enlightenment. Here it is used in the latter sense.

The term "Pratyeka-buddha" designates one who has attained enlightenment on his own without joining the religious order. Because of his selfish attitude and his unwillingness to help save the world, he also is regarded as an inferior sage in the polemical writings of Mahayana literature, though he is slightly higher than an Arhat. A Bodhisattva, who sacrifices himself for the world, is classified as higher than either of them.

The permeations of ignorance are of two kinds. One is the basic permeation, since it can put into operation the "activating mind," and the other is the permeation that de-velops perverse views and attachments, since it can put into operation the "object-discriminating consciousness."

b. Permeation of Suchness

How does the permeation [of Suchness] give rise to the pure state and continue uninterrupted? It may be said that there is the principle of Suchness, and it can permeate into ignorance. Through the force of this permeation, [Suchness] causes the deluded mind to loathe the suffering of samsara and to aspire for nirvana. Because this mind, though still de-luded, is [now] possessed with loathing and aspiration, it permeates into Suchness [in that it induces Suchness to mani-fest itself]. Thus a man comes to believe in his essential na-ture, to know that what exists is the erroneous activity of the mind and that the world of objects in front of him is nonexistent, and to practice teachings to free himself [from the erroneously conceived world of objects]. He knows what is really so—that there is no world of objects in front of him —and therefore with various devices he practices courses by which to conform [himself to Suchness]. He will not attach himself to anything nor give rise to any [deluded] thoughts. Through the force of this permeation [of Suchness] over a long period of time, his ignorance ceases. Because of the cessa-tion of ignorance, there will be no more rising of the [de-luded activities of] mind. Because of the nonrising [of the deluded activities of mind], the world of objects [as previ-ously conceived] ceases to be; because of the cessation of both the primary cause (ignorance) and the coordinating causes (objects), the marks of the [defiled] mind will all be nullified. This is called "gaining nirvana and accomplishing spontane-ous acts."

The permeation [of Suchness] into the deluded mind is of two kinds. The first is the permeation into the "object-discriminating consciousness." [Because of this permeation], ordinary men and the Hinayanists come to loathe the suffering of samsara, and thereupon each, according to his capacity, gradually advances toward the highest enlightenment (Ch., *tao*). The second is the permeation into mind. [Because of this permeation], Bodhisattvas advance to nirvana rapidly and with aspiration and fortitude.

Two kinds of permeation of Suchness [into ignorance] can be identified. The first is the "permeation through manifestation of the essence [of Suchness], and the second is "the permeation through [external] influences."

The phrase, "the permeation through manifestation of the essence [of Suchness]," can perhaps be rendered literally as "the permeation through manifestation of essence on its own accord." Following Fa-tsang's comment, this permeation has traditionally been understood as "internal permeation" (Ch., *nei-hsün*).[25] It is the inner urge of Suchness in man to emerge, so to speak, from the state of unawareness to the state of awareness, or from the unconscious to the conscious. It is an internal movement of Suchness within, from potential to actual, or from essence to existence, so that essence permeates into existence, or nirvana into samsara. Suchness within, i.e., original enlightenment, is constantly asserting itself in order to be actualized by breaking through the wall of ignorance. This intrinsic inner dynamics of Suchness is suggested by the term "internal permeation."

(1) *Permeation through Manifestation of the Essence of Suchness* [The essence of Suchness] is, from the beginningless beginning, endowed with the "perfect state of purity." It is provided with suprarational functions and the nature of manifesting itself. Because of these two reasons it permeates perpetually [into ignorance]. Through the force of [this permeation] it induces a man to loathe the suffering of samsara, to seek bliss in nirvana, and, believing that he has the principle of Suchness within himself, to make up his mind to exert himself.

"The perfect state of purity *(an-āsrava-dharma)*" is identified by Fa-tsang with "the original enlightenment of nonemptiness." [26] "The nature of manifesting itself." The original Chinese of this phrase can be literally translated as "the nature of making the world of object." Taken literally, the phrase makes little sense, though commentators have usually tried to take it that way. For example, T'an-yen (516–588), the oldest commentator whose work has been preserved, went so far as to interpret it as a magical creation of the objects of the senses.[27] Suchness, in an absolute sense, can never be an object or objects. When objectified, it is no longer the Absolute, but turns into a relative. "Making the world of object," therefore, should be taken symbolically as suggesting "revealing itself," "manifesting itself from within," etc. It does not objectify itself externally, but is internally asserting its absolute Subjectivity in man.

Question: If this is so, then all sentient beings are endowed with Suchness and are equally permeated by it. Why is it that there are infinite varieties of believers and nonbelievers, and that there are some who believe sooner and some later? All of them should, knowing that they are endowed with the principle of Suchness, at once make an effort utilizing expedient means and should all equally attain nirvana.

· Answer: Though Suchness is originally one, yet there are immeasurable and infinite [shades of] ignorance. From the very beginning ignorance is, because of its nature, characterized by diversity, and its degree of intensity is not uniform. Defilements, more numerous than the sands of the Ganges, come into being because of [the differences in intensity of] ignorance, and exist in manifold ways; defilements, such as the belief in the existence of atman and the indulgence in passion, develop because of ignorance and exist in different ways. All these defilements are brought about by ignorance, in an infinitely diversified manner in time. The Tathāgatas alone know all about this.

In Buddhism there is [a teaching concerning] the primary cause and the coordinating causes. When the primary cause and the coordinating causes are sufficiently provided, there will be the perfection [of a result]. It is like the case of wood: though it possesses a [latent] fire nature which is the primary cause of its burning, it cannot be made to burn by itself unless men understand the situation and resort to means [of actualizing fire out of wood by kindling it]. In the same way a man, though he is in possession of the correct primary cause, [Suchness with] permeating force, cannot put an end to his defilements by himself alone and enter nirvana unless he is provided with coordinating causes, i.e., his encounters with the Buddhas, Bodhisattvas, or good spiritual friends. Even though coordinating causes from without may be sufficiently provided, if the pure principle [i.e., Suchness] within is lacking in the force of permeation, then a man cannot ultimately loathe the suffering of samsara and seek bliss in nirvana. However, if both the primary and the coordinating causes are sufficiently provided, then because of his possession of the force of permeation [of Suchness from within] and the compassionate protection of the Buddhas and Bodhisattvas [from without], he is able to develop a loathing for suffering, to believe that nirvana is real, and to cultivate his capacity for goodness. And when his cultivation of the capacity for goodness matures, he will as a result meet the Buddhas and Bodhisattvas and will be instructed, taught, benefited, and given joy, and then he will be able to advance on the path to nirvana.

(2) *Permeation through Influences* This is the force from without affecting men by providing coordinating causes. Such external coordinating causes have an infinite number of meanings. Briefly, they may be explained under two categories: namely, the specific and the general coordinating causes.

(a) The Specific Coordinating Causes. A man, from the time when he first aspires to seek enlightenment until he

becomes an Enlightened One, sees or meditates on the Buddhas and Bodhisattvas [as they manifest themselves to him];
sometimes they appear as his family members, parents, or
relatives, sometimes as servants, sometimes as close friends, or
sometimes as enemies. Through all kinds of deeds and incalculable performances, such as the practice of the four acts
of loving-kindness, etc., they exercise the force of permeation
created by their great compassion, and are thus able to cause
sentient beings to strengthen their capacity for goodness and
are able to benefit them as they see or hear [about their
needs]. This [specific] coordinating cause is of two kinds.
One is immediate and enables a man to obtain deliverance
quickly; and the other is remote and enables a man to obtain
deliverance after a long time. The immediate and remote
causes are again of two kinds: the causes which strengthen
a man in his practices [of expedient means to help others],
and those which enable him to obtain enlightenment (Ch.,
tao).

Mahayanists interpreted the Śākyamuni Buddha as a temporal
incarnation in history of the Eternal Buddha, the Dharmakaya,
who appeared in order to help save the world. This theory made
it possible to postulate any number of temporal, but unhistorical,
manifestations of Buddhas and Bodhisattvas as the popularization
of Mahayana Buddhism progressed. In order to become a popular
religion, mythologization was inevitable. Perhaps the best example of this trend can be found in a section of the Lotus Sutra
in which the Bodhisattva Avalokiteśvara appears in all forms of
being in order to protect believers in all conceivable situations,
in the end leading them to enlightenment.[28]
   "The four acts of loving-kindness" are defined as charity, kind
speech, beneficial action, and cooperation.
   The translation follows Fa-tsang's interpretation.[29] Wŏnhyo says
concerning the "causes which strengthen a man in his practice,"
that "they develop various practices such as charity, observance
of precepts, etc." Concerning the causes "which enable him to
obtain enlightenment," he says that they are "those which develop [the intention on the part of the devotee] to hear [about

doctrines], to think [about them], and to practice [them], and thus [enable him] to obtain enlightenment." [30]

(b) The General Coordinating Causes. The Buddhas and Bodhisattvas all desire to liberate all men, spontaneously permeating them [with their spiritual influences] and never forsaking them. Through the power of the wisdom which is one [with Suchness], they manifest activities in response to [the needs of men] as they see and hear them. [Because of this indiscriminately permeating cause], men are all equally able, by means of concentration (samadhi), to see the Buddhas.

"The wisdom which is one [with Suchness]": Because the comments of Fa-tsang and others are too brief and vague at this point, the translation follows the interpretation of the Chinese monk, Tzu-hsüan (d. 1038). He says: "In essence, this wisdom is the same as Suchness," and also that "this [wisdom] enables one to know that all profane (ordinary men) and sacred (enlightened men), defiled and pure, are equally one in what is Real." [31]

This permeation through the influence of the wisdom whose essence is one [with Suchness] is also divided into two categories [according to the types of recipients].

The one is yet to be united [with Suchness]. Ordinary men, the Hinayanists, and those Bodhisattvas who have just been initiated devote themselves to religious practices on the strength of their faith, being permeated by Suchness through their mind and consciousness. Not having obtained the indiscriminate mind, however, they are yet to be united with the essence [of Suchness], and not having obtained [the perfection of] the discipline of free acts, they are yet to be united with the influence [of Suchness].

Fa-tsang identifies "[the perfection of] the discipline of free acts" with the "knowledge which emerges after enlightenment, and which functions spontaneously, adapting itself to all circumstances in the world." [32]

The other is the already united [with Suchness]: Bodhisattvas who realize Dharmakaya have obtained undiscriminating mind [and are united with the essence of the Buddhas; they, having obtained free acts,] [33] are united with the influence of the wisdom of the Buddhas. They singly devote themselves with spontaneity to their religious disciplines, on the strength of Suchness within; permeating into Suchness [so that Suchness will reclaim itself], they destroy ignorance.

Again, the defiled principle (dharma), from the beginningless beginning, continues perpetually to permeate until it perishes by the attainment of Buddhahood. But the permeation of the pure principle has no interruption and no ending. The reason is that the principle of Suchness is always permeating; therefore, when the deluded mind ceases to be, the Dharmakaya [i.e., Suchness, original enlightenment] will be manifest and will give rise to the permeation of the influence [of Suchness], and thus there will be no ending to it.

> That is to say, ignorance has no beginning but does have an ending; while original enlightenment, or Suchness, has neither beginning nor ending. It is evident that the nature of ignorance is not ontological but is epistemological. If it were ontological and were conceived as "being," this conclusion that ignorance has no beginning but has an ending would be absurd.

II. *The Essence Itself and the Attributes of Suchness, or The Meanings of Mahā* [34]

A. The Greatness of the Essence of Suchness

[The essence of Suchness] knows no increase or decrease in ordinary men, the Hinayanists, the Bodhisattvas, or the

Buddhas. It was not brought into existence in the beginning nor will it cease to be at the end of time; it is eternal through and through.

B. The Greatness of the Attributes of Suchness

From the beginning, Suchness in its nature is fully provided with all excellent qualities; namely, it is endowed with the light of great wisdom, [the qualities of] illuminating the entire universe, of true cognition and mind pure in its self-nature; of eternity, bliss, Self, and purity; of refreshing coolness, immutability, and freedom. It is endowed with [these excellent qualities] which outnumber the sands of the Ganges, which are not independent of, disjoined from, or different from [the essence of Suchness], and which are suprarational [attributes of] Buddhahood. Since it is endowed completely with all these, and is not lacking anything, it is called the *Tathāgata-garbha* [when latent] and also the Dharmakaya of the Tathāgata.

Question: It was explained before that the essence of Suchness is undifferentiated and devoid of all characteristics. Why is it, then, that you have described its essence as having these various excellent qualities?

Answer: Though it has, in reality, all these excellent qualities, it does not have any characteristics of differentiation; it retains its identity and is of one flavor; Suchness is solely one.

Question: What does this mean?

Answer: Since it is devoid of individuation, it is free from the characteristics of individuation; thus, it is one without any second.

Question: Then how can you speak of differentiation [i.e., the plurality of the characteristics of Suchness]?

Answer: In [contrast to] the characteristics of the phenomena of the "activating mind" [the characteristics of Suchness can] be inferred.

The translation of the last sentence follows in the main the interpretation of Fa-tsang.[35] Literally, "we show it, depending on the characteristics of birth and death of the activating mind." This means that though, in the ultimate sense, Suchness defies any predication of its characteristics, the characteristics of Suchness can be symbolically suggested in relative terms that are accessible to the deluded mind, and are imagined to be the exact opposites of the characteristics of phenomena of the "activating mind."

Question: How can they be inferred?

Answer: All things are originally of the mind only; they in fact transcend thoughts.[36] Nevertheless, the deluded mind, in nonenlightenment, gives rise to [irrelevant] thoughts and predicates the world of objects. This being the case, we define [this mentality] as "the state of being destitute of wisdom (*avidyā*: ignorance)." The essential nature of Mind is immutable [in that it does not give rise to any deluded thoughts, and, therefore, is the very opposite of ignorance]; hence, [it is spoken of as having the characteristic of] "the light of great wisdom."

When there is a particular perceiving act of the mind, objects [other than the objects being perceived] will remain unperceived. The essential nature of Mind is free from any partial perceiving; hence, [Suchness is spoken of as having the characteristic of] "illuminating the entire universe."

When the mind is in motion [stirred by ignorance], it is characterized by illusions and defilements, outnumbering the sands of the Ganges, such as lack of true cognition, absence of self-nature, impermanence, blisslessness, impurity, fever, anxiety, deterioration, mutation, and lack of freedom. By contrast to this, the essential nature of Mind, however, is motionless [i.e., undisturbed by ignorance]; therefore, it can be inferred that it must have various pure and excellent qualities, outnumbering the sands of the Ganges. But if the mind gives rise to [irrelevant thoughts] and further predicates the world of objects, it will continue to lack [these qualities]. All these numberless excellent qualities of the pure principle are none other than those of One Mind, and there is nothing to be sought after anew by thought. Thus, that which is fully endowed with them is called the Dharmakaya [when manifested] and the *Tathāgata-garbha* [when latent].

c. The Greatness of the Influences of Suchness

The Buddha-Tathāgatas, while in the stages of Bodhisattvahood, exercised great compassion, practiced *pāramitās,* and accepted and transformed sentient beings. They took great vows, desiring to liberate all sentient beings through countless aeons until the end of future time, for they regarded all sentient beings as they regarded themselves. And yet, they never regarded them as [separate] sentient beings. Why? Because they truly knew that all sentient beings and they themselves were identical in Suchness and that there could be no distinction between them.

"*Pāramitās*": Requirements to be perfected by sentient beings who are potentially enlightened, i.e., by Bodhisattvas in order to attain enlightenment. They are means to be practiced by the Mahayanists in order to cross over from this shore of samsara to the other shore of nirvana. The so-called six *pāramitās* are most frequently encountered in Mahayana literature. They are: charity, observance of precepts (of nonkilling, nonstealing, nonadultery, etc.), patience, zeal, meditation, and wisdom.

The type of paradoxical expression that we meet with here can most frequently be found in the Wisdom literature. To cite an example similar to the one in our text, a passage from the

Diamond Sutra (*Vajracchedikā*) which belongs to the body of Wisdom literature says:

> The Lord said: Here, Subhuti, someone who has set out in the vehicle of a Bodhisattva should produce a thought in this manner: "As many beings as there are in the universe of beings, comprehended under the term 'beings' . . . all these I must lead to Nirvana, into that Realm of Nirvana which leaves nothing behind. And yet, although innumerable beings have thus been led to Nirvana, no being at all has been led to Nirvana." And why? If in a Bodhisattva the notion of a "being" should take place, he could not be called a "Bodhi-being." "And why? He is not to be called a Bodhi-being, in whom the notion of a self or of a being should take place, or the notion of a living soul or of a person." [37]

Because they possessed such great wisdom [which could be applied] to expedient means [in quest of enlightenment], they extinguished their ignorance and perceived the original Dharmakaya. Spontaneously performing incomprehensible activities, exercising manifold influences, they pervade everywhere in their identity with Suchness. Nevertheless, they reveal no marks of their influences that can be traced as such. Why? Because the Buddha-Tathāgatas are no other than the Dharmakaya itself, and the embodiment of wisdom. [They belong to the realm of] the absolute truth, which transcends the world where the relative truth operates. They are free from any conventional activities. And yet, because of the fact that sentient beings receive benefit through seeing or hearing about them, their influences [i.e., of Suchness] can be spoken of [in relative terms].

The double standards of truth, one being the "absolute truth" and the other the "relative truth," have played an important role in Mahayana Buddhism. The explanations of the double sets of truth vary from school to school, but we can find a classical exposition of them in Nāgārjuna. His verses on the topic read as follows:

> Elucidation of the dharma (doctrine) of the Buddha is on the basis of twofold truth: one is the worldly truth (*samvriti-*

satya), and the other, the ultimate truth (paramārtha-satya).
Those who do not know the distinction between these two
types of truth do not know the profound truth (tattva) in
the instruction of the Buddha.

The ultimate truth is not to be shown except on the basis of
the conventional truth (vyavahāra-satya); without gaining
the ultimate truth nirvana is not to be obtained.[38]

The ultimate truth is the truth of the ultimately Real, i.e., Suchness, nirvana, etc., which may be experienced but which is
devoid of any empirical determinations. On the other hand, the
relative truth, or conventional truth, is the empirical truth accepted by people in the world and can be communicated by
the use of language; in this category are scientific truths, the
truths of social ethics, etc. One is the truth of the Absolute order,
and the other, that of the phenomenal order.

The influences [of Suchness] are of two kinds. The first is
that which is conceived by the mind of ordinary men and the
followers of Hinayana [i.e., the influence of Suchness as re-
flected] in the "object-discriminating consciousness." This is
called [the influence of Suchness in the form of] the "Transformation-body" (Nirmanakaya). Because they do not know
that it is projected by the "evolving mind," they regard it as
coming from without; they assume that it has a corporeal
limitation because their understanding is limited.

The second is that which is conceived by the mind of the
Bodhisattvas, from the first stage of aspiration to the highest
stage, [i.e., the influence of Suchness as reflected] in the mentality which regards external objects as unreal.[39] This is called
[the influence of Suchness in the form of] the "Bliss-body"
(Sambhogakaya). It has an infinite number of corporeal
forms, each form has an infinite number of major marks, and
each major mark has an infinite number of subtle marks.
The land where it has its abode has innumerable adornments. It manifests itself without any bounds; [its manifestations are] inexhaustible and free from any limitations. It
manifests itself in accordance with the needs [of sentient

beings]; and yet it always remains firm without destroying or losing itself. These excellent qualities were perfected by the pure permeation acquired by the practice of *pāramitās* and the suprarational permeation [of Suchness]. Since the influence is endowed with infinite attributes of bliss, it is spoken of as the "Bliss-body."

The "major marks (*lakshana*)" are usually regarded as the thirty-two auspicious physical signs visible on the body of the Buddha or universal monarch, such as the halo, the white curl emitting light between the eyebrows, etc. The "subtle marks (*anu-vyañjana*)" are generally regarded as the eighty minor marks of the Buddha or Bodhisattva, such as long, thin, shining fingernails.

What is seen by ordinary men is only the coarse corporeal forms [of the manifestation of Suchness]. Depending upon where one is in the six transmigratory states, his vision of it will differ. [The visions of it conceived by] the unenlightened beings are not in a form of Bliss; this is the reason why it is called the "Transformation-body" [i.e., the body appearing in the likeness of the conceiver].

One of the most important concepts in Mahayana Buddhism, which appears in this section dealing with the influences of Suchness, is the theory of the Triple Body of the Buddha, the three aspects of which are known as the Dharmakaya, the Sambhogakaya, and the Nirmanakaya. The *Awakening of Faith* is known, among other things, for its concise presentation of this theory. As presented in the text, the Dharmakaya or "Essence-body" represents the manifested form of pure Suchness, which in its latent form is known as the *Tathāgata-garbha*. The Sambhogakaya or "Bliss-body" represents Suchness as conceived by the mind of the Bodhisattvas, endowed with infinite attributes of bliss. The Nirmanakaya or "Transformation-body" represents Suchness as conceived by the minds of ordinary people, the body appearing in the likeness of the conceiver.

"The six transmigratory states" are the states of being or worlds to which sentient beings are led by the force of the karma which they have created in their previous lives. These states are those of: dwellers in hell, hungry ghosts, beasts, vicious fighting spirits (*asura*), human beings, and gods (*deva*). All of them are subject to transmigration, being in the order of samsara.

The Bodhisattvas in their first stage of aspiration and the others, because of their deep faith in Suchness, have a partial insight into [the nature of the influence of Suchness]. They know that the things [of the Bliss-body], such as its corporeal forms, major marks, adornments, etc., do not come from without or go away, that they are free from limitations, and that they are envisioned by mind alone and are not independent of Suchness. These Bodhisattvas, however, are not free from dualistic thinking, since they have yet to enter into the stage [where they gain complete realization] of the Dharmakaya. If they advance to the "stage of pure-heartedness," [the forms] they see will be subtler and the influences [of Suchness] will be more excellent than ever. When they leave the last stage of Bodhisattvahood, they will perfect their insight [into Suchness]. When they become free from the "activating mind" they will be free from the perceiving [of duality]. The Dharmakaya of the Buddhas knows no such thing as distinguishing this from that.

This is a repeated theme that the "process of actualization of enlightenment is the process of integrating the identity with the original enlightenment." The direction of the process can be suggested by the following illustration:
Essence > existence > essence; nirvana > samsara > nirvana; potential > unawareness of the potential + partial awareness > actualization of the potential; or Absolute order > phenomenal order > Absolute order. The process is a flight of Suchness to Suchness; nirvana to nirvana; Buddha to Buddha.

Question: If the Dharmakaya of the Buddhas is free from the manifestation of corporeal form, how can it appear in corporeal form?

Answer: Since the Dharmakaya is the essence of corporeal form, it is capable of appearing in corporeal form. The reason this is said is that from the beginning corporeal form and Mind have been nondual. Since the essential nature of corporeal form is identical with wisdom, the essence of corporeal form which has yet to be divided into tangible forms is called the "wisdom-body." Since the essential nature of wisdom is identical with corporeal form, [the essence of corporeal form which has yet to be divided into tangible forms] is called Dharmakaya pervading everywhere. Its manifested corporeal forms have no limitations. It can be freely manifested as an infinite number of Bodhisattvas, Buddhas of Bliss-body, and adornments in the ten quarters of the universe. Each of them has neither limitation nor interference. All of these are incomprehensible to the dualistic thinking of the [deluded] mind and consciousness, for they result from the free influence of Suchness.

> The foregoing discussion would seem to suggest the familiar concept, so often found in creation myths or in rituals of magic practice, that "to think is to create." Essentially, however, it is different in that these manifestations are visions which are conceived in accordance with the mind; that is, they depend on the mentality of the devotee. What is really noteworthy is the statement that "from the beginning corporeal form (*rūpa*; Ch., *sê*) and mind have been nondual (*advaya*; Ch., *pu-erh*)." The nonduality of mind and matter, spirit and body is the basic concept of this text and a common presupposition of Mahayana Buddhism.

III. *From Samsara to Nirvana*

Lastly, how to enter into the realm of Suchness from the realm of samsara will be revealed. Examining the five components, we find that they may be reduced to matter (object) and mind (subject). The objects of the five senses and of the mind are in the final analysis beyond what they are thought to be. And the mind itself is devoid of any form or mark and is, therefore, unobtainable as such, no matter where one may seek it. Just as a man, because he has lost his way, mistakes the east for the west, though the actual directions have not changed place, so people, because of their ignorance, assume Mind (Suchness) to be what they think it to be, though Mind in fact is unaffected [even if it is falsely predicated]. If a man is able to observe and understand that Mind is beyond what it is thought to be, then he will be able to conform to and enter the realm of Suchness.

"The five components (skandhas)": The constituents of all physical and mental states. In early Buddhism, particularly in the Hinayana School called Sarvāstivādin ("one who asserts that everything is"), they were believed to be real. They are: matter (rūpa), feeling (vedanā), ideation (samjñā), predisposition (samskāra), and consciousness (vijñāna).

For "beyond what they are thought to be," the original has wu-nien, which literally means "no-thought." Wu-nien is used in the text in the sense of "beyond empirical predication or determination," and probably corresponds to a Sanskrit term a-cintya (unthinkable) or a-vikalpya (unanalyzable by intellect). At first glance, this section seems to be disappointingly short and elusive. However, what else could have been said about the problem? The solution lies in personal experience rather than in verbal description. The purport of the paragraph, however, is clear: the knowledge which is relevant within the framework of the subject-object relationship—in other words, the dualistic mentality—must be transcended in order to gain the vision of Suchness and to reinstate oneself in the Absolute order.

CHAPTER TWO

The Correction of Evil Attachments

In this chapter, an attempt is made to refute false doctrines so that the assertion made in the preceding chapter may prove to be correct. The content of this chapter is not suggested in the Outline, but to refute irrelevant views is an indispensable step.

All evil attachments originate from biased views; if a man is free from bias, he will be free from evil attachments. There are two kinds of biased view: one is the biased view held by those who are not free from the belief in atman [i.e., ordinary men]; the other is the biased view held by those who believe that the components of the world are real [i.e., the Hinayanists].

"Biased views" is not a literal translation; the original reads *wo-chien,* usually understood as indicating a wrong speculative theory which holds that atman is real. From the following context, however, it is obvious that *wo-chien* is not used in this ordinary sense, but denotes "biased or subjective or irrelevant views."

I. *The Biased Views Held by Ordinary Men*

There are five kinds of biased views held by ordinary men which may be discussed.

Hearing that it is explained in the sutra that the Dharmakaya of the Tathāgata is, in the final analysis, quiescent, like empty space, ordinary men think that the nature of the Tathāgata is, indeed, the same as empty space, for they do not know [that the purpose of the sutra is] to uproot their adherence.

"Quiescent" is literally "tranquil and desolate (*chi-mo*)," which suggests a state of complete absence of being. The purpose of stating that the Dharmakaya is "quiescent, like empty space," is to negate the adherence to the notion that the Dharmakaya is a Being, a kind of anthropomorphic being among beings in the universe. On the other hand, to believe that the Dharmakaya is literally nonbeing is a wrong view. This error leads to an adherence to the notion of nonbeing as a form of being.[40]

Question: How is this to be corrected?

Answer: [The way to correct this error is] to understand clearly that "empty space" is a delusive concept, the substance of which is nonexistent and unreal. It is merely predicated in relation to [its correlative] corporeal objects. If it is taken as a being [termed nonbeing, a negative being, then it should be discarded, because] it causes the mind to remain in samsara. In fact there are no external corporeal objects, because all objects are originally of the mind. And as long as there are no corporeal objects at all, "empty space" cannot be maintained. All objects are of the mind alone; but when illusions arise, [objects which are regarded as real] appear. When the mind is free from its deluded activities, then all objects [imagined as real] vanish of themselves. [What is real,] the one and true Mind, pervades everywhere. This is the final meaning of the Tathāgata's great and comprehensive wisdom. [The Dharmakaya is, indeed,] unlike "empty space."

> "Nonbeing" is inconceivable when there is no "being." In other words, "non-a" cannot be talked about when there is no "a"; death is meaningless in the absence of life, or vice versa. Seen from the point of view of the Absolute order—though this view is in practice possible only for the Enlightened Ones—the phenomenal order simply does not exist. The Absolute order is unlike "empty space," which needs a correlative for its existence. Because of its transcendental nature and, at the same time, because of its immanent nature of Suchness it is symbolically said that "the one true Mind pervades everywhere."

Hearing that it is explained in the sutra that all things in the world, in the final analysis, are empty in their substance, and that nirvana or the principle of Suchness is also absolutely empty from the beginning and devoid of any characteristics, they, not knowing [that the purpose of the sutra is] to uproot their adherence, think that the essential nature of Suchness or nirvana is simply empty.

Question: How is this to be corrected?

Answer: [The way to correct this error is] to make clear that Suchness or the Dharmakaya is not empty, but is endowed with numberless excellent qualities.

This is a refutation of nihilism. Concerning this biased view, Fa-tsang says, "It is an erroneous adherence to the notion that the essence of Suchness (dharma) is absolute nothingness (k'ung-wu)." [41] Since the essence of Suchness cannot be predicated, it is called śūnya (empty); but if a man takes it as literally true, he takes a position in nihilism, another extreme and false view. Though Suchness defies predication, it can be suggested symbolically by such terms as compassion, light, life, etc.

Hearing that it is explained in the sutra that there is no increase or decrease in the *Tathāgata-garbha* and that it is provided in its essence with all excellent qualities, they, not being able to understand this, think that in the *Tathāgata-garbha* there is plurality of mind and matter.

Question: How is this to be corrected?

Answer: [They should be instructed that the statement in the sutra that "there is no increase or decrease in the *Tathā-gata-garbha*"] is made only in accordance with the [absolute] aspect of Suchness, and [the statement that "it is provided with all excellent qualities"] is made in accordance with [the pluralistic outlook held by the defiled minds in] samsara.

Fa-tsang says: "In accordance with the [absolute] aspect of Suchness" stands for "the nonduality of the dual (the nonduality of Absolute and phenomena)," and "in accordance with the pluralistic outlook held by the defiled minds in samsara" stands for "the duality of the nondual (phenomena on the ground of the Absolute)." [42]

Hearing that it is explained in the sutra that all defiled states of samsara in the world exist on the ground of the

Tathāgata-garbha and that they are therefore not independent of Suchness, they, not understanding this, think that the *Tathāgata-garbha* literally contains in itself all the defiled states of samsara in the world.

Question: How is this to be corrected?

[In order to correct this error it should be understood that] the *Tathāgata-garbha,* from the beginning, contains only pure excellent qualities which, outnumbering the sands of the Ganges, are not independent of, severed from, or different from Suchness; that the soiled states of defilement which, outnumbering the sands of the Ganges, merely exist in illusion; are, from the beginning, nonexistent; and from the beginningless beginning have never been united with the *Tathāgata-garbha*. It has never happened that the *Tathāgata-garbha* contained deluded states in its essence and that it induced itself to realize [Suchness] in order to extinguish forever its deluded states.

This is an argument as to whether Suchness contains in itself evils or whether evils are a part of Suchness. To this the answer is given: evils are not a part of Suchness, for they are not "own-beings"; their appearance is due not to Suchness but to a deluded mind on the part of man. If evils were a part of Suchness, how could Suchness help to extinguish evils?

Hearing that it is explained in the sutra that on the ground of the *Tathāgata-garbha* there is samsara as well as the attainment of nirvana, they, without understanding this, think that there is a beginning for sentient beings. Since they suppose a beginning, they suppose also that the nirvana attained by the Tathāgata has an end and that he will in turn become a sentient being.

Question: How is this to be corrected?

Answer: [The way to correct this error is to explain that] the *Tathāgata-garbha* has no beginning, and that therefore ignorance has no beginning. If anyone asserts that sentient beings came into existence outside this triple world, he holds the view given in the scriptures of the heretics. Again, the *Tathāgata-garbha* does not have an end; and the nirvana attained by the Buddhas, being one with it, likewise has no end.

The misunderstanding lies in mistaking logical conditioning for a time order as to which comes first and which comes later. When any two terms—for example, ignorance and enlightenment, samsara and nirvana, good and evil—are incorrectly thought to be absolutely exclusive polarities, one may fall into the error of supposing that they alternate in time. The assumption in the text is that on the logical ground of the original enlightenment, ignorance appears; on the ground of nirvana, samsara exists. Fa-tsang says of this: "Hearing that an illusion is dependent on what is true, they think that what is true exists first and then illusion comes later. Thus they have come to entertain a wrong view that there is a beginning. [Or in reverse order,] like a certain heretic who claims that from the original darkness emerges enlightenment, they think that there is a beginning to being a sentient being [i.e., an original fall into the order of samsara] and then [an escape from there] depending on what is true." [43]

II. *The Biased Views Held by the Hinayanists*

Because of their inferior capacity, the Tathāgata preached to the Hinayanists only the doctrine of the nonexistence of atman and did not preach his doctrines in their entirety; as a result, the Hinayanists have come to believe that the five components, the constituents of samsaric existence, are real; being terrified at the thought of being subject to birth and death, they erroneously attach themselves to nirvana.

Question: How is this to be corrected?

Answer: [The way to correct this error is to make clear that] the five components are unborn in their essential nature and, therefore, are imperishable—that [what is made of the five components] is, from the beginning, in nirvana.

Nirvana is conceived by the Hinayanists as a state of perfect annihilation; i.e., as nonbeing, in contrast to being, which undergoes constant transformation.

"Unborn (an-utpanna; Ch., pu-sheng)" is a paradoxical expression suggesting the transcendence of both being and nonbeing, one of the most fundamental ideas of Mahayana Buddhism. Pu-sheng, when used as an adjective, denotes "unborn," "uncreated," "unproduced," etc., and as a noun (an-utpāda or an-utpatti) "no-birth," "no-creation," "no-production," etc. The popularity of the expression undoubtedly owes much to the opening stanza of Nāgārjuna's Mādhyamaka-kārikās, declaring the eightfold negation, which begins: "Imperishable, unborn (an-utpāda). . . ." "Unborn" or "uncreated" is not a concept diametrically opposed to its counterpart "born" or "created," but belongs to a higher order transcending the dichotomy of both being and nonbeing, birth and death, eternalism and nihilism, etc. Thus it is used almost interchangeably with śūnyatā, advaya (nondual), nih-svabhāva (no-self-substance), etc.

Finally, in order to be completely free from erroneous attachments, one should know that both the defiled and the pure states are relative and have no particular marks of their own-being that can be discussed. Thus, all things from the beginning are neither matter nor mind, neither wisdom nor consciousness, neither being nor non-being; they are ultimately inexplicable. And yet they are still spoken of. It should be understood that the Tathāgatas, applying their expedient means, make use of conventional speech in a provisional manner in order to guide people, so that they can be free from their deluded thoughts and can return to Suchness; for if anyone thinks of anything [as real and absolute in its own right], he causes his mind to be [trapped] in samsara and consequently he cannot enter [the state filled with] true insight [i.e., enlightenment].

The iconoclastic nature of Mahayana Buddhism with regard to the ultimate validity of language is clearly in evidence here, where the dangers involved in the absolutization of the relative are cautioned against. The term "defiled state" here refers to the concepts of samsara, evil, ignorance, being, nonbeing, etc.; while "pure state" refers to the Absolute, good, enlightenment, nirvana, etc.

It may appear strange to negate even wisdom, the acquirement of which is thought to be the only means by which one can destroy ignorance. But wisdom, when solidified as a certain view, turns into a type of knowledge, a product of the analytical mind which only functions dualistically in terms of subject and object relationships. In this sense, wisdom should also be transcended, just as *śūnyatā*, taken as a view among views, must be negated.

CHAPTER THREE

Analysis of the Types of Aspiration for Enlightenment, or The Meanings of Yāna[44]

All Bodhisattvas aspire to the enlightenment (*bodhi;* Ch., *tao*) realized by all the Buddhas, disciplining themselves to this end, and advancing toward it. Briefly, three types of aspiration for enlightenment can be distinguished. The first is the aspiration for enlightenment through the perfection of faith. The second is the aspiration for enlightenment through understanding and through deeds. The third is the aspiration for enlightenment through insight.

I. *The Aspiration for Enlightenment through the Perfection of Faith*

Question: By whom and through what kind of discipline can faith be perfected so that the aspiration for enlightenment may be developed?

Answer: Among those who belong to the group of the undetermined, there are some who, by virtue of their excellent capacity for goodness developed through permeation, believe in the [law of] retribution of karma and observe the ten precepts. They loathe the suffering of samsara and wish to seek the supreme enlightenment. Having been able to meet the Buddhas, they serve them, honor them, and practice the faith. Their faith will be perfected after ten thousand aeons. Their aspiration for enlightenment will be developed either through the instruction of the Buddhas and the Bodhisattvas, or because of their great compassion [toward their suffering fellow beings], or from their desire to preserve the good teaching from extinction. Those who are thus able to develop their aspiration through the perfection of faith will enter the group of the determined and will never retrogress. They are called the ones who are united with the correct cause [for enlightenment] and who abide among those who belong to the Tathāgata family.

"The group of the undetermined": Those who have not established an unretrogressive faith, i.e., those who repeatedly advance and retreat in the course of attaining enlightenment; or in mythological terms, those who have not received the assurance of attaining enlightenment by a certain Buddha.

The exact nature of the "ten precepts" differs in the different traditions of Buddhism. The following ten are popularly accepted in the Mahayana tradition of the Far East: not to kill, not to steal, not to commit adultery, not to lie, not to use flowery words, not to slander, not to be double-tongued, not to covet, not to give way to anger, not to harbor biased views.

"Aeon" is a translation of the Sanskrit kalpa, a unit of time, often said to be the time it would take for a celestial maiden who comes down to the earth once every hundred years to wear away an immense rock by brushing it with her sleeve. Such expressions, needless to say, should be taken symbolically. They are used sometimes in order to suggest the extreme difficulty of establishing correct faith, or sometimes to convey an entirely new

sense of dimension. Often a qualitative difference is expressed
by an extremely exaggerated quantitative expression.

There are, however, people [among those who belong to
the group of the undetermined] whose capacity for goodness
is slight and whose defilements, having accumulated from
the far distant past, are deep-rooted. Though they may also
meet the Buddhas and honor them, they will develop the potentiality merely to be born as men, as dwellers in heaven, or
as followers of the Hinayana. Even if they should seek after
the Mahayana, they would sometimes progress and sometimes regress because of the inconsistent nature of their capacity. And also there are some who honor the Buddhas and
who, before ten thousand aeons have passed, will develop an
aspiration because of some favorable circumstances. These
circumstances may be the viewing of the Buddhas' corporeal
forms, the honoring of monks, the receiving of instructions
from the followers of the Hinayana, or the imitation of
others' aspiration. But these types of aspiration are all inconsistent, for if the men who hold them meet with unfavor-
able circumstances, they will relapse and fall back into the
stage of attainment of the followers of the Hinayana.

Now, in developing the aspiration for enlightenment
through the perfection of faith, what kind of mind is to
be cultivated? Briefly speaking, three kinds can be discussed.
The first is the mind characterized by straightforwardness,
for it correctly meditates on the principle of Suchness. The
second is the mind of profoundness, for there is no limit to
its joyful accumulation of all kinds of goodness. The third
is the mind filled with great compassion, for it wishes to
uproot the sufferings of all sentient beings.

Question: Earlier it has been explained that the World
of Reality is one, and that the essence of the Buddhas has
no duality. Why is it that people do not meditate [of their

own accord] on Suchness alone, but must learn to practice good deeds?

Answer: Just as a precious gem is bright and pure in its essence but is marred by impurities, [so is a man.] Even if he meditates on his precious nature, unless he polishes it in various ways by expedient means, he will never be able to purify it. The principle of Suchness in men is absolutely pure in its essential nature, but is filled with immeasurable impurity of defilements. Even if a man meditates on Suchness, unless he makes an effort to be permeated by it in various ways by applying expedient means, he certainly cannot become pure. Since the state of impurity is limitless, pervading throughout all states of being, it is necessary to counteract and purify it by means of the practice of all kinds of good deeds. If a man does so, he will naturally return to the principle of Suchness.

As to the expedient means, there are, in short, four kinds:

The first is the fundamental means to be practiced. That is to say, a man is to meditate on the fact that all things in their essential nature are unborn, divorcing himself from deluded views so that he does not abide in samsara. [At the same time] he is to meditate on the fact that all things are [the products of] the union of the primary and coordinating causes, and that the effect of karma will never be lost. [Accordingly] he is to cultivate great compassion, practice meritorious deeds, and accept and transform sentient beings equally without abiding in nirvana, for he is to conform himself to [the functions of] the essential nature of Reality (*dharmatā*) which knows no fixation.

The last clause in the immediately preceding paragraph, "for he is to conform himself to . . . ," can literally be translated as "because he is to follow the nonabiding of the essential nature of Reality (*dharmatā*)." The term "nonabiding (*a-pratiṣṭha*)" suggests freedom, spontaneity, nonattachment, nondogmatism, etc. It is a way of life, a practical application of "emptiness (*śūnyatā*)" in a life situation encompassing both intellectual and affectional aspects.

In this paragraph, three ideas are presented: First, faith in the Absolute order; second, the legitimate recognition of the phenomenal order where the law of causality operates; third, the synthesis of these two orders in a way of life for men.

The second is the means of stopping [evils]. The practice of developing a sense of shame and repentance can stop all evils and prevent them from growing, for one is to conform oneself to the faultlessness of the essential nature of Reality.

The third is the means of increasing the capacity for goodness that has already been developed. That is to say, a man should diligently honor and pay homage to the Three Treasures, and should praise, rejoice in, and beseech the Buddhas. Because of the sincerity of his love and respect for the Three Treasures, his faith will be strengthened and he will be able to seek the unsurpassed enlightenment. Furthermore, being protected by the *Buddha,* the *Dharma,* and the *Sangha,* he will be able to wipe out the hindrances of evil karma. His capacity for goodness will not retrogress because he will be conforming himself to the essential nature of Reality, which is free from hindrances produced by stupidity.

The fourth is the means of the great vow of universal salvation. This is to take a vow that one will liberate all sentient beings, down to the last one, no matter how long it may take to cause them to attain the perfect nirvana, for one will be conforming oneself to the essential nature of Reality which is characterized by the absence of discontinuity. The essential nature of Reality is all-embracing, and pervades all sentient beings; it is everywhere the same and one without duality; it does not distinguish this from that, because it is, in the final analysis, in the state of quiescence.

When a Bodhisattva develops this aspiration for enlightenment [through faith], he will be able, to a certain extent, to realize the Dharmakaya. Because of this realization of the Dharmakaya, and because he is led by the force of the vow [that he made to liberate all sentient beings], he is able to present eight types of manifestation of himself for the benefit of all sentient beings. These are: the descent from the Tushita heaven; the entrance into a human womb; the stay in the womb; the birth; the renunciation; the attainment of enlightenment; the turning of the wheel of the Dharma (doctrine); and the entrance into nirvana. However, such a Bodhisattva cannot be said [to have perfectly realized] the Dharmakaya, for he has not yet completely destroyed the outflowing evil karma which has been accumulated from his numberless existences in the past. He must suffer some slight misery deriving from the state of his birth. However, this is due not to his being fettered by karma, but to his freely made decision to carry out the great vow [of universal salvation in order to understand the suffering of others].

"The eight types of manifestation" reflect the historio-mythic account of the life of Śākyamuni Buddha. In the usual account, however, a phase called the "subduing of Māra, the tempter," appears after "the renunciation," and "the stay in the womb" is omitted. "To turn the wheel of the Dharma" means to preach. The first sermon of the Buddha at Benares is known as "the turning of the wheel of the Dharma." The form given here is commonly known as the "eight types of manifestation of Mahayana."

It is said in a sutra that there are some [Bodhisattvas of this kind] who may regress and fall into evil states of existence, but this does not refer to a real regression. It says this merely in order to frighten and stir the heroism of the newly initiated Bodhisattvas who have not yet joined the group of the determined, and who may be indolent.

Furthermore, as soon as this aspiration has been aroused

in the Bodhisattvas, they leave cowardice far behind them and are not afraid even of falling into the stage of the followers of the Hinayana. Even though they hear that they must suffer extreme hardship for innumerable aeons before they may attain nirvana, they do not feel any fear, for they believe and know that from the beginning all things are of themselves in nirvana.

II. *The Aspiration for Enlightenment through Understanding and Deeds*

It should be understood that this type of aspiration is even more excellent than the former. Because the Bodhisattvas [who cherish this aspiration] are those who are about to finish the first term of the incalculable aeons since the time when they first had the correct faith, they have come to have a profound understanding of the principle of Suchness and to entertain no attachment to their attainments obtained through discipline.

Knowing that the essential nature of Reality is free from covetousness, they, in conformity to it, devote themselves to the perfection of charity. Knowing that the essential nature of Reality is free from the defilements which originate from the desires of the five senses, they, in conformity to it, devote themselves to the perfection of precepts. Knowing that the essential nature of Reality is without suffering and free from anger and anxiety, they, in conformity to it, devote themselves to the perfection of forbearance. Knowing that the essential nature of Reality does not have any distinction of body and mind and is free from indolence, they, in conformity to it, devote themselves to the perfection of zeal. Knowing that the essential nature of Reality is always calm and free from confusion in its essence, they, in conformity to it, devote themselves to the perfection of meditation. Knowing that the essential nature of Reality is always characterized by gnosis and is free from ignorance, they, in conformity to it, devote themselves to the perfection of wisdom.

III. *The Aspiration for Enlightenment through Insight*

[As for the Bodhisattvas of this group, who range] from the "stage of pure-heartedness" to the "last stage of Bodhisattvahood," what object do they realize? They realize Suchness. We speak of it as an object because of the "evolving mind," but in fact there is no object in this realization [that can be stated in terms of a subject-object relationship]. There is only the insight into Suchness [transcending both the seer and the seen]; we call [this the experience of] the Dharmakaya.

The "evolving mind (*pravritti-vijñāna*)" is that which, because of ignorance, emerges as the perceiving and thinking subject. The implication of the sentence is that, though Suchness cannot be predicated, when explanation is needed there is no other way but to use relative terms that are accessible to the mind which functions only in terms of subject-object relationships.

The Bodhisattvas of this group can, in an instant of thought, go to all worlds of the universe, honor the Buddhas, and ask them to turn the wheel of the Dharma. In order to guide and benefit all men, they do not rely on words. Sometimes, for the sake of weak-willed men, they show how to attain perfect enlightenment quickly by skipping over the stages [of the Bodhisattva]. And sometimes, for the sake of indolent men, they say that men may attain enlightenment at the end of numberless aeons. Thus they can demonstrate innumerable expedient means and suprarational feats. But in reality all these Bodhisattvas are the same in that they are alike in their lineage, their capacity, their aspiration, and their realization [of Suchness]; therefore, there is no such thing as skipping over the stages, for all Bodhisattvas must pass through the three terms of innumerable aeons [before they can fully attain enlightenment]. However, because of the differences in the various worlds of beings, and in the objects of seeing and hearing, as well as in the capacity, desires, and nature of the various beings, there are also different ways of teaching them what to practice.

The opening sentence in this paragraph that ends with "the Dharma" is a symbolic presentation of the suprarational influences of Suchness, i.e., Dharmakaya. Since the Bodhisattvas who have realized the Dharmakaya are one with Suchness, they are thought to function in accordance with the mysterious functions of Suchness. It also corresponds to the spontaneous action of saving others after attaining enlightenment.

The clause, "they do not rely on words (*pu-yi wen-tzu*)" is ambiguous. Fa-tsang and other commentators give us no clue to the meaning. In the later translation of the *Awakening of Faith,* made by Śikshānanda, this clause is replaced by the words, "they do not seek to hear any melodious sounds or words," [45] which would seem to imply that the Bodhisattvas devote themselves to the salvation of mankind and do not remain in heaven enjoying the celestial music and songs—another way of saying that they do not stay in the bliss of nirvana. The statement that "they do not rely on words" is close in spirit to the claim of Zen Buddhism that the "transmission of Zen does not rely on words but is from mind to mind." Here, in view of what follows, the statement would seem to mean that the Bodhisattvas do not cling to literal interpretations of the scriptures, but are ready to interpret them freely, accommodating their interpretation to all possible situations of suffering beings, with the single aim of helping them to advance to the way of salvation.

The characteristics of the aspiration for enlightenment entertained by a Bodhisattva belonging to this group can be identified in terms of the three subtle modes of mind. The first is the true mind, for it is free from [false intellectual] discrimination. The second is the mind [capable] of [applying] expedient means, for it pervades everywhere spontaneously and benefits sentient beings. The third is the mind [subject to the influence] of karma [operating] in subconsciousness, for it appears and disappears in the most subtle ways.

> Of these "three subtle modes of mind," Fa-tsang says: "The true mind is the basic wisdom free from discrimination [of subject and object]. The mind of expedient means is the wisdom which, after having obtained enlightenment, functions spontaneously to help save others. The third, the subconsciousness, is the Storehouse Consciousness which is the basis of these other two kinds of wisdom." [46]
>
> If the third is the Storehouse Consciousness, as Fa-tsang says, then the expression "appearing and disappearing," literally "birth and cessation," is the characterization of the Storehouse Consciousness, which is explained by Vasubandhu as being analogous to the flow of a river that changes from moment to moment and yet retains its identity. [47] The implication may be that, though these Bodhisattvas are enlightened and actively engaged in the work of helping others, they have yet to be perfected, being subject to the influence of the "activating mind," which is stirred by ignorance in the Storehouse Consciousness.

Again, a Bodhisattva of this group, when he brings his excellent qualities to perfection, manifests himself in the heaven of Akanishta as the highest physical being in the world. Through wisdom united with [original enlightenment or Suchness] in an instant of thought, he suddenly extinguishes ignorance. Then he is called [the one who has obtained] all-embracing knowledge. Performing suprarational acts spontaneously, he can manifest himself everywhere in the universe and benefit all sentient beings.

> "The heaven of Akanishta" is the highest heaven in the world of form, according to the cosmology of Indian Buddhism.

Question: Since space is infinite, worlds are infinite. Since worlds are infinite, beings are infinite. Since beings are infinite, the variety of their mentalities must also be infinite. The objects of the senses and the mind must therefore be limitless, and it is difficult to know and understand them all. If ignorance is destroyed, there will be no thoughts in the mind. How then can a comprehension [that has no content] be called "all-embracing knowledge"?

Answer: All objects are originally of One Mind and are beyond thought determination. Because unenlightened people perceive objects in their illusion, they impose limitations in their mind. Since they erroneously develop these thought determinations, which do not correspond to Reality (*dharmatā*), they are unable to reach any inclusive comprehension. The Buddha-Tathāgatas are free from all perverse views and thoughts [that block correct vision; therefore,] there are no corners into which their comprehension does not penetrate. Their Mind is true and real; therefore, it is no other than the essential nature of all things. [The Buddhas], because of their very nature, can shed light on all objects conceived in illusion. They are endowed with an influence of great wisdom [that functions as the application] of innumerable expedient means. Accommodating themselves to the capacity of understanding of various sentient beings, they can reveal to them the manifold meanings of the doctrine. This is the reason they may be called those who have "all-embracing knowledge."

Question: If the Buddhas are able to perform spontaneous acts, to manifest themselves everywhere, and to benefit all sentient beings, then the sentient beings should all be able, by seeing their physical forms, by witnessing their miracles, or by hearing their preachings, to gain benefit. Why is it then that most people in this world have not been able to see the Buddhas?

Answer: The Dharmakaya of all the Buddhas, being one and the same everywhere, is omnipresent. Since the Buddhas are free from any fixation of thought, their acts are said to be "spontaneous." They reveal themselves in accordance with the mentalities of all the various sentient beings. The mind of the sentient being is like a mirror. Just as a mirror cannot reflect images if it is coated with dirt, so the Dharmakaya cannot appear in the mind of the sentient being if it is coated with the dirt [of defilements].

PART

4

On Faith and Practice

Having already discussed interpretation, we will now present a discussion of faith and practice. This discussion is intended for those who have not yet joined the group of beings who are determined to attain enlightenment.

On Four Faiths

Question: What kind of faith [should a man have] and how should he practice it?

Answer: Briefly, there.are four kinds of faith. The first is the faith in the *Ultimate Source*. Because [of this faith] a man comes to meditate with joy on the principle of Suchness. The second is the faith in the numberless excellent qualities of the *Buddhas*. Because [of this faith] a man comes to meditate on them always, to draw near to them in fellowship, to honor them, and to respect them, developing his capacity for goodness and seeking after the all-embracing knowledge. The third is the faith in the great benefits of the *Dharma* (Teaching). Because [of this faith] a man comes constantly to re-

member and practice various disciplines leading to enlightenment. The fourth is the faith in the *Sangha* (Buddhist Community) whose members are able to devote themselves to the
practice of benefiting both themselves and others. Because
[of this faith] a man comes to approach the assembly of
Bodhisattvas constantly and with joy and to seek instruction
from them in the correct practice.

The word "Bodhisattva" does not here refer to beings such as
Manjuśrī, Avalokiteśvara, etc., but to any sentient being who is
intrinsically enlightened but who has yet to actualize the original enlightenment, and who is making an effort to this end.

On Five Practices

There are five ways of practice which will enable a man to
perfect his faith. They are the practices of charity, [observ-
ance of] precepts, patience, zeal, and cessation [of illusions]
and clear observation.

Question: How should a man practice charity?

Answer: If he sees anyone coming to him begging, he
should give him the wealth and other things in his possession
in so far as he is able; thus, while freeing himself from greed
and avarice, he causes the beggar to be joyful. Or, if he sees
one who is in hardship, in fear, or in grave danger, he should
give him freedom from fear in so far as he is able. If a man
comes to seek instruction in the teaching, he should, according to his ability and understanding, explain it by the use
of expedient means. In doing so, however, he should not
expect any fame, material gain, or respect, but he should
think only of benefiting himself and others alike and of ex-
tending the merit [that he gains from the practice of charity]
toward the attainment of enlightenment.

Question: How should he practice the [observance of] precepts?

Answer: He is not to kill, to steal, to commit adultery, to be double-tongued, to slander, to lie, or to utter exaggerated speech. He is to free himself from greed, jealousy, cheating, deceit, flattery, crookedness, anger, hatred, and perverse views. If he happens to be a monk [or nun] who has renounced family life, he should also, in order to cut off and suppress defilements, keep himself away from the hustle and bustle of the world and, always residing in solitude, should learn to be content with the least desire and should practice vigorous ascetic disciplines. He should be frightened and filled with awe by any slight fault and should feel shame and repent. He should not take lightly any of the Tathāgata's precepts. He should guard himself from slander and from showing dislike so as not to rouse people in their delusion to commit any offense or sin.

Question: How should he practice patience?

Answer: He should be patient with the vexatious acts of others and should not harbor thoughts of vengeance, and he should also be patient in matters of gain or loss, honor or dishonor, praise or blame, suffering or joy, etc.

Question: How should he practice zeal?

Answer: He should not be sluggish in doing good, he should be firm in his resolution, and he should purge himself of cowardice. He should remember that from the far distant past he has been tormented in vain by all of the great sufferings of body and mind. Because of this he should diligently practice various meritorious acts, benefiting himself and others, and liberate himself quickly from suffering. Even if a man practices faith, because he is greatly hindered by the evil karma derived from the grave sins of previous lives, he may be troubled by the evil Tempter (Māra) and his demons, or entangled in all sorts of worldly affairs, or afflicted by the suffering of disease. There are a great many hindrances of this kind. He should, therefore, be courageous and zealous, and at the six four-hour intervals of the day and night should pay homage to the Buddhas, repent with sincere heart, beseech the Buddhas [for their guidance], rejoice in the happiness of others, and direct all the merits [thus acquired] to the attainment of enlightenment. If he never abandons these practices, he will be able to avoid the various hindrances as his capacity for goodness increases.

Question: How should he practice cessation and clear observation?

Answer: What is called "cessation" means to put a stop to all characteristics (*lakshana*) of the world [of sense objects and of the mind], because it means to follow the *samatha* (tranquility) method of meditation. What is called "clear observation" means to perceive distinctly the characteristics of the causally conditioned phenomena (samsara), because it means to follow the *vipaśyanā* (discerning) method of meditation.

Question: How should he follow these?

Answer: He should step by step practice these two aspects and not separate one from the other, for only then will both be perfected.

These two methods of meditation, i.e., *samatha* (Ch., *chih*) and *vipaśyanā* (Ch., *kuan*), singly and also as a pair, appear in the scriptures of old Pāli sources. Much discussion of them is to be found in the sutras and commentaries. Explanations differ, but the basic notion that *samatha* implies "tranquilization, stabilization, cessation, etc.," and that *vipaśyanā* implies "discerning, clear observation, distinct perception, etc." remains unchallenged. The most elaborate descriptions of them are to be found in the T'ien-t'ai School of Buddhism in China.[48]

The Practice of Cessation

Should there be a man who desires to practice "cessation," he should stay in a quiet place and sit erect in an even temper. [His attention should be focused] neither on breathing nor on any form or color, nor on empty space, earth, water, fire, wind, nor even on what has been seen, heard, remembered, or conceived. All thoughts, as soon as they are conjured up, are to be discarded, and even the thought of discarding them is to be put away, for all things are essentially [in the state of] transcending thoughts, and are not to be created from moment to moment nor to be extinguished from moment to moment; [thus one is to conform to the essential nature of Reality (*dharmatā*) through this practice of cessation].[49] And it is not that he should first meditate on the objects of the senses in the external world and then negate them with his mind, the mind that has meditated on them. If the mind wanders away, it should be brought back and fixed in "correct thought." It should be understood that this "correct thought" is [the thought that] whatever is, is mind only and that there is no external world of objects [as conceived]; even this mind is devoid of any marks of its own [which would indicate its substantiality] and therefore is not substantially conceivable as such at any moment.[50]

Even if he arises from his sitting position and engages in other activities, such as going, coming, advancing, or standing still, he should at all times be mindful [of the application] of expedient means [of perfecting "cessation"], conform [to the immobile principle of the essential nature of Reality],[51] and observe and examine [the resulting experiences]. When this discipline is well mastered after a long period of practice, [the ideations of] his mind will be arrested. Because of this, his power of executing "cessation" will gradually be intensified and become highly effective, so that he will conform himself to, and be able to be absorbed into, the "concentration (samadhi) of Suchness." Then his defilements, deep though they may be, will be suppressed and his faith strengthened; he will quickly attain the state in which there will be no retrogression. But those who are skeptical, who lack faith, who speak ill [of the teaching of the Buddha], who have committed grave sins, who are hindered by their evil karma, or who are arrogant or indolent are to be excluded; these people are incapable of being absorbed into [the samadhi of Suchness].

Next, as a result of this samadhi, a man realizes the oneness of the World of Reality (*dharmadhātu*), i.e., the sameness everywhere and nonduality of the Dharmakaya of all the Buddhas and the bodies of sentient beings. This is called "the samadhi of one movement." [52] It should be understood that [the samadhi of] Suchness is the foundation of [all other] samadhi. If a man keeps practicing it, then he will gradually be able to develop countless other kinds of samadhi.

If there is a man who lacks the capacity for goodness, he will be confused by the evil Tempter, by heretics and by demons. Sometimes these beings will appear in dreadful forms while he is sitting in meditation, and at other times they will manifest themselves in the shapes of handsome men and women. [In such a case] he should meditate on [the principle of] "mind only," and then these objects will vanish and will not trouble him any longer. Sometimes they may appear as the images of heavenly beings or Bodhisattvas, and assume also the figure of the Tathāgata, furnished with all the major and minor marks; or they may expound the spells or preach charity, the precepts, patience, zeal, meditation, and wisdom; or they may discourse on how the true nirvana is the state of universal emptiness, of the nonexistence of characteristics, vows, hatreds, affections, causes, and effects; and of absolute nothingness. They may also teach him the knowledge of his own past and future states of existence, the method of reading other men's minds, and perfect mastery of speech, causing him to be covetous and attached to worldly fame and profit; or they may cause him to be frequently moved to joy and anger and thus to have unsteadiness of character, being at times very kind-hearted, very drowsy, very ill, or lazy-minded; or at other times becoming suddenly zealous, and then afterward lapsing into negligence; or developing a lack of faith, a great deal of doubt, and a great deal of anxiety; or abandoning his fundamental excellent practices [toward religious perfection] and devoting himself to miscellaneous religious acts, or being attached to worldly affairs which involve him in many ways; or sometimes they may cause him to experience a certain semblance of various kinds of samadhi, which are all the attainments of heretics and are not the true samadhi; or sometimes they may cause him to remain in samadhi for one, two, three, or up to seven days, feeling comfort in his body and joy in his mind, being neither hungry nor thirsty, partaking of natural, fragrant, and delicious drinks and foods, which induce him to increase his attachment to them; or at other times they may cause him to eat without any restraint, now a great deal, now only a little, so that the color of his face changes accordingly.

For these reasons, he who practices ["cessation"] should be discreet and observant, lest his mind fall into the net of evil [doctrine]. He should be diligent in abiding in "correct thought," neither grasping nor attaching himself to [anything]; if he does so, he will be able to keep himself far away from the hindrance of these evil influences.

He should know that the samadhi of the heretics are not free from perverse views, craving, and arrogance, for the heretics are covetously attached to fame, profit, and the re-spect of the world. The samadhi of Suchness is the samadhi in which one is not arrested by the activity of viewing [a subject] nor by the experiencing of objects [in the midst of meditation]; even after concentration one will be neither indolent nor arrogant and one's defilements will gradually decrease. There has never been a case in which an ordinary man, without having practiced this samadhi, was still able to join the group that is entitled to become Tathāgatas. Those who practice the various types of dhyana (meditation) and samadhi which are popular in the world will develop much attachment to their flavors and will be bound to the triple world because of their perverse view that atman is real. They are therefore the same as heretics, for as they depart from the protection of their good spiritual friends, they turn to heretical views.

Next, he who practices this samadhi diligently and whole-heartedly will gain ten kinds of advantages in this life. First, he will always be protected by the Buddhas and the Bodhisat-tvas of the ten directions. Second, he will not be frightened by the Tempter and his evil demons. Third, he will not be deluded or confused by the ninety-five kinds of heretics[53] and wicked spirits. Fourth, he will keep himself far away from slanders of the profound teaching [of the Buddha], and will gradually diminish the hindrances derived from grave sins. Fifth, he will destroy all doubts and wrong views on enlightenment. Sixth, his faith in the Realm of the Tathāgata will grow. Seventh, he will be free from sorrow and remorse and in the midst of samsara will be full of vigor and undaunted. Eighth, having a gentle heart and forsaking arrogance, he will not be vexed by others. Ninth, even if he has not yet experienced samadhi, he will be able to decrease his defilements in all places and at all times, and

he will not take pleasure in the world. Tenth, if he ex-
periences samadhi, he will not be startled by any sound from
without.

Now, if he practices "cessation" only, then his mind will
be sunk [in self-complacency] and he will be slothful; he
will not delight in performing good acts but will keep himself far away from the exercise of great compassion. It is,
therefore, necessary to practice "clear observation" [as well].

The Practice of Clear Observation

He who practices "clear observation" should observe that
all conditioned phenomena in the world are unstationary
and are subject to instantaneous transformation and destruction; that all activities of the mind arise and are extinguished
from moment to moment; and that, therefore, all of these
induce suffering. He should observe that all that had been
conceived in the past was as hazy as a dream, that all that is
being conceived in the present is like a flash of lightning,
and that all that will be conceived in the future will be like
clouds that rise up suddenly. He should also observe that
the physical existences of all living beings in the world are
impure and that among these various filthy things there is
not a single one that can be sought after with joy.

He should reflect in the following way: all living beings,
from the beginningless beginning, because they are permeated by ignorance, have allowed their mind to remain in
samsara; they have already suffered all the great miseries of
the body and mind, they are at present under incalculable
pressure and constraint, and their sufferings in the future
will likewise be limitless. These sufferings are difficult to
forsake, difficult to shake off, and yet these beings are unaware

[that they are in such a state]; for this, they are greatly to be pitied.

After reflecting in this way, he should pluck up his courage and make a great vow to this effect: may my mind be free from discriminations so that I may practice all of the various meritorious acts everywhere in the ten directions; may I, to the end of the future, by applying limitless expedient means, help all suffering sentient beings so that they may obtain the bliss of nirvana, the ultimate goal.

Having made such a vow, he must, in accordance with his capacity and without faltering, practice every kind of good at all times and at all places and not be slothful in his mind. Except when he sits in concentration in the practice of "cessation," he should at all times reflect upon what should be done and what should not be done.

Whether walking, standing, sitting, lying, or rising, he should practice both "cessation" and "clear observation" side by side. That is to say, he is to meditate upon the fact that things are unborn in their essential nature; but at the same time he is to meditate upon the fact that good and evil karma, produced by the combination of the primary cause and the co-ordinating causes, and the retributions [of karma] in terms of pleasure, pain, etc., are neither lost nor destroyed. Though he is to meditate on the retribution of good and evil karma produced by the primary and coordinating causes [i.e., he is to practice "clear observation"], he is also to meditate on the fact that the essential nature [of things] is unobtainable [by intellectual analysis]. The practice of "cessation" will enable ordinary men to cure themselves of their attachments to the world, and will enable the followers of the Hinayana to forsake their views, which derive from cowardice. The practice of "clear observation" will cure the followers of the Hinayana of the fault of having narrow and inferior minds which bring forth no great compassion, and will free ordinary men from their failure to cultivate the capacity for goodness. For these reasons, both "cessation" and "clear observation" are complementary and inseparable. If the two are not practiced together, then one cannot enter the path to enlightenment.

Next, suppose there is a man who learns this teaching for the first time and wishes to seek the correct faith but lacks courage and strength. Because he lives in this world of suffering, he fears that he will not always be able to meet the Buddhas and honor them personally, and that, faith being difficult to perfect, he will be inclined to fall back. He should know that the Tathāgatas have an excellent expedient means by which they can protect his faith: that is, through the strength of wholehearted meditation on the Buddha, he will in fulfillment of his wishes be able to be born in the Buddha-land beyond, to see the Buddha always, and to be forever separated from the evil states of existence. It is as the sutra says: "If a man meditates wholly on Amitābha Buddha in the world of the Western Paradise and wishes to be born in that world, directing all the goodness he has cultivated [toward that goal], then he will be born there." [54] Because he will see the Buddha at all times, he will never fall back. If he meditates on the Dharmakaya, the Suchness of the Buddha, and with diligence keeps practicing [the meditation], he will be able to be born there in the end because he abides in the correct samadhi.[55]

Encouragement
of Practice and the Benefits Thereof

As has already been explained in the preceding sections, the Mahayana is the secret treasury of the Buddhas. Should there be a man who wishes to obtain correct faith in the profound Realm of the Tathāgata and to enter the path of Mahayana, putting far away from himself any slandering [of the teaching of Buddha], he should lay hold of this treatise, deliberate on it, and practice it; in the end he will be able to reach the unsurpassed enlightenment.

If a man, after having heard this teaching, does not feel any fear or weakness, it should be known that such a man is certain to carry on the lineage of the Buddha and to receive the prediction of the Buddha that he will obtain enlightenment. Even if a man were able to reform all living beings throughout all the systems in the universe and to induce them to practice the ten precepts, he still would not be superior to a man who reflects correctly upon this teaching even for the time spent on a single meal, for the excellent, qualities which the latter is able to obtain are unspeakably superior to those which the former may obtain.

If a man takes hold of this treatise and reflects on and practices [the teachings given in it] only for one day and one night, the excellent qualities he will gain will be boundless and indescribable. Even if all the Buddhas of the ten directions were to praise these excellent qualities for incalculably long periods of time, they could never reach the end of their praise, for the excellent qualities of the Reality (*dharmatā*) are infinite and the excellent qualities gained by this man will accordingly be boundless.

If, however, there is a man who slanders and does not believe in this treatise, for an incalculable number of aeons he will undergo immense suffering for his fault. Therefore all people should reverently believe in it and not slander it, [for slander and lack of faith] will gravely injure oneself as well as others and will lead to the destruction of the lineage of the Three Treasures.

Through this teaching all Tathāgatas have gained nirvana, and through the practice of it all Bodhisattvas have obtained Buddha-wisdom. It should be known that it was by means of this teaching that the Bodhisattvas in the past were able to perfect their pure faith; that it is by means of this teaching that the Bodhisattvas of the present are perfecting their pure faith; and that it is by means of this teaching that the Bodhisattvas of the future will perfect their pure faith. Therefore men should diligently study and practice it.[56]

Profound and comprehensive are the great principles of the Buddha,
Which I have now summarized as faithfully as possible.
May whatever excellent qualities I have gained from this endeavor
In accordance with Reality be extended for the benefit of all beings.

NOTES

Notes to Introduction

1. T32, pp. 575–83 (No. 1666). The Taisho edition of the Chinese Tripitaka will henceforward be abbreviated as T.

2. Part One: The Reasons for Writing; cf: translation p. 27.

3. Edward Conze: *Buddhist Wisdom Books* (London, George Allen and Unwin, 1958), p. 101.

4. Mochizuki Shinkō, one of the modern specialists on the text, in a work written in 1922 identified 176 commentaries. Since he included two English translations and a commentary on the later version of the text as translated by Śikshānanda, this figure, to be exact, should be reduced to 173 in his listings. Cf. his *Daijō kishin-ron no kenkyū* (Study of the *Awakening of Faith in the Mahayana*) (Tokyo, 1922), pp. 201–346.

5. The most sound and comprehensive study on these problems can be found in Paul Demiéville's article, "Sur l'authenticité du Ta Tch'ing K'i Sin Louen," *Bulletin de la Maison Franco-Japonaise*, II (no. 2, 1929), 1–78. Also recommended is an article by Walter Liebenthal, "New Light on the Mahāyāna-śraddhotpāda śāstra": *T'oung Pao*, XLVI (1958), 155–216. His approach is radical; he suggests that Tao-ch'ung (476?–550?) might have been the author (*ibid.*, pp. 210–15). In addition, consult the articles written by modern Chinese Buddhist scholars and collected

in a book, edited by Shih T'ai-hsŭ, entitled *Ta-ch'eng ch'i-hsin lun chên-wei pien* (Wu-ch'ang, China, 1923). The book contains nine articles representing both radical and conservative approaches.

6. The *Buddhacarita* is the most famous work of Aśvaghosha. It is the finest work of the entire Buddhist literature in this genre. In the Sanskrit manuscripts only about half of the epic has been preserved; therefore, translations into Western languages done from Sanskrit contain the account of the life of Buddha from his birth to the attainment of enlightenment only, and not to his last day on earth. The missing half can be supplied from Chinese and Tibetan translations of the missing Sanskrit portions. For those who are interested, a selected bibliography of the translations into Western languages follows:

From Sanskrit: 1. E. B. Cowell: *The Buddha-karita of Aśvaghosha,* Vol. 49 of the *Sacred Books of the East.* Oxford, 1894. 2. Carl Cappeller: *Buddha's Wandel.* Jena, 1922. 3. Richard Schmidt: *Buddha's Leben.* Hanover, 1923. 4. E. H. Johnston: *The Buddhacarita or, Acts of the Buddha, Part II.* Calcutta, 1936. *From Chinese:* Samuel Beal: *A Life of Buddha by Aśvaghosha Bodhisattva* (translated from Sanskrit into Chinese by Dharmaraksha, A.D. 420). Vol. 19 of the *Sacred Books of the East.* Oxford, 1883. *From Tibetan:* Friedrich Weller: *Das Leben des Buddha von Aśvaghosha.* 2 vols. Leipzig, 1926–28.

7. The *Saundarananda* is an epic on the conversion to Buddhism of a handsome young man named Nanda. Though there is no Chinese or Tibetan translation, the Sanskrit manuscripts have been preserved, and there is a good English translation by E. H. Johnston: *The Saundarananda or Nanda the Fair* (Oxford University Press, 1932).

8. This work, though fragmentary, is significant as being the earliest evidence of dramatic literature in India. It is written partly in Sanskrit and partly in dialects in accordance with the standard style of old Indian drama. The different dialects are spoken by persons such as women and servants and reflect the social status of these characters.

9. T32, p. 594bc.

10. *Zoku-zōkyō,* Part I, Case 71, Vol. 3, pp. 264–80.

11. Walter Liebenthal, "The Oldest Commentary of the Mahāyānaśraddhotpāda Śāstra," *Bukkyō bunka kenkyū* (Studies in Buddhism and Buddhist civilization), Nos. 6, 7 (Kyoto, 1958), p. 7.

12. T55, p. 142a.

13. T32, pp. 584–91.

14. This information is found in the introduction to the new translation of the text, and is probably a much later addition. Cf. T32, p. 583c.

15. Mochizuki Shinkō, *Daijō kishin-ron no kenkyū*, p. 99.

16. T50, p. 458b.

17. Those who are interested in the comparative study of the two texts in the original can find a systematic presentation of similarities and differences in the following article: Kashiwagi Hiroo, "Shikushananda no yaku to tsutaerareru Daijō kishin-ron (On the translation of the Awakening of Faith in the Mahayana attributed to Śikshānanda)," *Journal of Indian and Buddhist Studies*, X (No. 2, March, 1962), 124–25.

18. T44, pp. 175–201.

19. T44, pp. 202–26.

20. T44, pp. 240–87.

21. Mochizuki Shinkō, *Daijō kishin-ron no kenkyū*, pp. 255–56.

22. T32, pp. 591–668.

23. Cf. Takamine Ryōshū, *Kegon shisō shi* (History of Hua-yen thought) (Kyoto, 1962), p. 64; and Kobayashi Jitsugen, "Kishin-ron kaishaku no hensen (Transitions in the interpretations of the *Awakening of Faith*)," *Journal of Indian and Buddhist Studies*, XIII (No. 2, March, 1965), 225–28.

24. This short essay is recommended for students of Chinese thought and religion in general, as it deals with both Confucianism and Taoism from the Buddhist point of view. The characteristic pattern of later Chinese Buddhism, syncretism, is remarkably evidenced in this. It has been said that Tsung-mi wrote this treatise in reply to the denunciation of Buddhism by Han Yü (768–824), one of the noted champions of Confucianism in the T'ang period. Cf. *Kegon shisō* (Hua-yen thought), edited by Kawada Kumatarō and Nakamura Hajime (Kyoto, 1960), p. 507. It has been translated into French and German but not as yet into English. Cf. Paul Masson-Oursel, trans., "Le Yuan Jen

Louen," *Journal Asiatique,* May–April, 1915, pp. 4–58; Heinrich Dumoulin, "Genninron, Tsungmi's Traktat vom Ursprung des Menschen," *Monumenta Nipponica,* I, 178–221.

25. Cf. *Zoku-zōkyō,* Part I, Case 14, Vol. 3, Tsung-mi's *Yüan-chüeh-ching ta-shu shih-yi ch'ao,* p. 277c.

26. Cf. Tsukamoto Zenryū: "Min-shin seiji no bukkyō kyosei (Emasculation of Buddhism by the Ming and the Ch'ing governments)," *Bukkyō Bunka Kenkyū* (The journal of Buddhistic culture), No. 2 (1952), p. 2.

27. T44, 243b.

28. Cf. D. T. Suzuki, trans., *The Lankavatara Sutra* (London, 1932).

29. This text has been translated from Tibetan. Cf. E. Obermiller, trans., "The Sublime Science of Buddhist Monism," *Acta Orientalia,* Vol. IX, Parts, 1, 2, 3, 1931.

30. E. H. Johnston, ed., *Ratnagotara-vibhāga-mahāyanottara-tantra-śāstra* (Patna, 1950), p. vii. Words within brackets are those supplied by the present translator.

31. Detailed information on the system can be obtained from such recent publications as: Tamaki Kōshirō, "The Development of the Thought of Tathāgata-garbha from India to China," *Journal of Indian and Buddhist Studies,* IX (No. 1, January 1961), 378–86; Katsumata Shunkyō, *Bukkyō ni okeru shinshiki-setsu no kenkyū* (A study of the Citta-vijñāna thought in Buddhism) (Tokyo, 1961), pp. 593–637; Mizutani Kōshō, "Nyoraizō shisō shi kenkyū josetsu (An introduction to the study of the history of Tathāgata-garbha thought)," *Bukkyō Daigaku kenkyū kiyō,* XLIV–XLV (Kyoto, 1963), 245–77; Ui Hakuju, *Hōshōron no kenkyū* (The study of the Ratnagotra-śāstra) (Tokyo, 1947).

32. Suzuki Teitaro (D. T. Suzuki), trans., *Aśvaghosha's Discourse on the Awakening of Faith in the Mahayana* (Chicago, 1900).

33. Rev. Timothy Richard, trans., *The Awakening of Faith in the Mahayana Doctrine—the New Buddhism* (Shanghai, 1907).

34. Dwight Goddard, ed., *A Buddhist Bible* (New York, 1952), pp. 357–404.

35. Timothy Richard, *The Awakening of Faith in the Mahayana Doctrine,* p. vi.

36. Dwight Goddard, *A Buddhist Bible*, Appendix, pp. 668–69. In the same section of the Appendix (p. 668), there is mention of one more English translation of which the present translator has no knowledge: "Another was made by several Sanskrit scholars from a Sanskrit text remade from the Chinese, and misses the profound esoteric significance of the original. This was published in the magazine, The Shrine of Wisdom, in 1929 and 1930."

Notes to Text

1. This pattern of analysis in terms of essence (Ch., *t'i*), attribute (or manifestation, appearance, etc.; Ch., *hsiang*), and influence (or function, activity, etc.; Ch., *yung*) is one of the great contributions that the *Awakening of Faith* has made to later Far Eastern thinkers. To cite an example: The master Kūkai (774–835), the founder of Shingon Buddhism in Japan, made use of this pattern as a basis in systematizing his religious philosophy. *Sokushin jōbutsu gi* (On attaining enlightenment with this very body), *Kōbō daishi zenshū*, Vol. I (Tokyo and Kyoto, 1910), pp. 507–8. The pattern of analysis in terms of essence and influence is found in the *Chao-lun* of Seng-chao (374–414). Cf. Tsukamoto Zenryū, ed., *Jōron kenkyū* (Kyoto, 1955), p. 200.

2. T44, p. 251b.

3. *Mādhyamaka-kārikās* XXV, 19.

4. Of the phrase, "all phases of existence in their totality," Dōgen (1200–53), the founder of Japanese Sōtō Zen, says: "In the one World of Reality, the essence (the Absolute) and appearances (phenomena) are inseparable and birth and death cannot be spoken about. There is nothing which is not of the essential nature of Mind, including even enlightenment and nirvana. All existences, the entire [range of] phenomena, are of the One Mind alone, and nothing is excluded. All these manifold phases of existences are equally of the One Mind and none differs from it. To discuss it in this manner is, indeed, an indication that a Buddhist really understands the essential nature of Mind. This being truly so, how can one falsely divide this One Reality into

body and mind and into samsara and nirvana?" Dōgen, *Bendōwa, Shōbō genzō* (Iwanami Edition) (Tokyo, 1942), pp. 69–70.

5. T44, p. 252b (adapted).

6. *Mādhyamaka-kārikās* XVIII, 7.

7. T44, p. 207b.

8. T44, p. 252c.

9. The statement that the *Tathāgata-garbha* is of *śūnya* and *a-śūnya* is found in the *Śrīmālā Sūtra,* a fact which suggests that this text developed the thought earlier expressed in that sutra. T12, p. 221c.

10. Innumerable expressions of a similar nature can be found in sutras that place emphasis on "emptiness" (*śūnyatā*) and also in the sayings of Buddhist masters, particularly those of the Zen school. For example, a Japanese Zen master Takuan (1573–1645) has this to say: "All phenomena are like phantoms or dreams; when it is once perceived that they are essentially empty, one does not see any particular marks of individuation in them and thus is free from attachments to them. In order to preclude attachments, this view of the emptiness of everything is taught. When this view is thoroughly realized, attachments will be severed. Having achieved this and on again returning to the world, one will find that there are no particulars to be destroyed and no attachment to be severed. . . ." Takuan, *Tōkai yawa, Takuan oshō zenshū,* Vol. 5 (Tokyo, 1929), p. 19.

11. *Mādhyamaka-kārikās* XXIV, 11.

12. An almost identical expression can be found in the *Śrīmālā Sūtra,* which is one of the representative works of the *Tathāgata-garbha* thought: "Oh, Lord, samsara (birth and death) is grounded on the *Tathāgata-garbha.* . . ." T12, p. 222b.

13. I have not been able to identify the source of this quotation.

14. The use of the term, the "reproducing mind (*khyāti-vijñāna*)," as well as the "object-discriminating consciousness (*vastu-prativikalpa-vijñāna*)," which will appear later in the text, is known to be peculiar to the *Laṅkāvatāra Sūtra.* This piece of evidence, among others, may indicate the influence of the sutra on this text. Cf. D. T. Suzuki: *Studies in the Lankavatara Sutra* (London, 1930; reprinted 1957), pp. 189–91.

15. The corresponding line in the commentary is found in T26, p. 169a.

16. *Daśabhūmika Sūtra,* ed. J. Rahder (Paris, 1926), p. 49; ed. R. Kondō (Tokyo, 1936), p. 98.

17. T44, pp. 214c–215a.

18. T44, p. 267a.

19. *Zoku-zōkyō,* Part I, Case 71, Vol. 5, p. 456d.

20. Proposed by Itō Kazuo. Cf. Itō Kazuo: *Shinchi no tankyū* (The Search for True Wisdom) (Kyoto, 1947), p. 46.

21. T44, p. 360c.

22. T44, p. 216a.

23. T44, p. 269a.

24. The idea and simile expressed in this paragraph somewhat correspond to a few passages in the *Lankāvatāra Sūtra.* Cf. D. T. Suzuki: *The Lankavatara Sutra* (London, 1932), p. 42.

25. T44, p. 271c.

26. T44, p. 271c.

27. *Zoku-zōykō,* Part I, Case 71, Vol. 3, p. 280a.

28. Cf. for example *the Lotus of the True Law,* trans. by H. Kern (Sacred Books of the East, Vol. XXI) (New York, Dover, 1963), pp. 406–18.

29. T44, p. 272c.

30. T44, p. 218a.

31. T44, p. 372b.

32. T44, p. 273a.

33. The passage within the brackets is missing in the text of the Taisho Tripitaka. The missing passage was supplied from the commentary of Fa-tsang (T44, p. 273a) and Koyasan University Edition (1955).

34. Headings in this section do not exist in the original. In order to clarify the discussion, the traditional practice of supplying these headings has been adopted, using the commentaries of Fa-tsang (T44, p. 273b) and of Wŏnhyo (T44, p. 218b) as a basis.

35. T44, p. 273c.

36. The original for "transcend thoughts" is *wu-yŭ-nien,* literally, "not to be in thoughts." This implies that all things are beyond what they are thought to be by the unenlightened mind, namely, they are not real, since they are falsely predicated by the deluded mind alone. In other words, Reality defies any thought determinations.

37. Edward Conze, trans., *Buddhist Wisdom Books* (London, 1958), p. 25.

38. *Mādhyamaka-kārikās* XXIV, 8, 9, 10.

39. Following the interpretation of Fa-tsang (T44, p. 275b). The latter part of the sentence reads literally, "depending on the activating mind." The use of the term "activating mind" here is very strange, a typical example of the inconsistent use of technical terms.

40. T44, p. 276c.

41. T44, p. 276c.

42. T44, p. 277b.

43. T44, p. 277b.

44. This chapter is an analysis of the meaning of the word *yāna* in the compound *Mahāyāna* given in the Outline.

45. T32, p. 589c.

46. T44, p. 280c.

47. Vasubhandhu: *Trimśikā* 4.

48. Chih-i (539–97), the founder of the T'ien-t'ai School in China, had enthusiastically emphasized the importance of these two methods of meditation as the foundation of all Buddhist practices. There are two books on meditation written by him which contain the words *chih-kuan* or "cessation and observation" in their titles. One is the *Mo-ho Chih-kuan* (Larger chih-kuan) (T46, pp. 1–140) in ten volumes; the other, the *Hsiao chih-kuan* (Smaller chih-kuan) (T46, pp. 462–73) in one volume; both have exerted a lasting influence in the Far East.

49. The portion in brackets is added to clarify the nature of this meditation and is based on the comment of Fa-tsang. Cf. T44, p. 283b.

50. The two sentences starting with "if the mind wanders away . . ." are quoted by Chih-i in the *Hsiao chih-kuan* (T46, p. 467a) as authority to support his assertions concerning meditation. Because of Chih-i's citation, the *Awakening of Faith* has been highly esteemed in the T'ien-t'ai tradition. A recent critical study of the textual tradition of the *Hsiao chih-kuan* has, however, revealed that this famous quotation was a later accretion. Cf. Sekiguchi Shindai, *Tendai shōshikan no kenkyū* (A study of the T'ien-t'ai *Hsiao Chih-kuan*) (Tokyo, 1953), pp. 282, 302–3, 307–10.

51. The portions in brackets are based upon Fa-tsang's interpretation. Cf. T44, p. 283c.

52. *Eka-caryā samādhi* (Ch., *i-hsing san-mei*)—the absorption

into the Absolute—was first introduced in the Wisdom Sutras and has played an important role in Far Eastern Buddhism. In the T'ien-t'ai tradition it is known as one of the four basic samadhi as defined by Chih-i; in the Pure Land School, it was advocated by Shan-tao (618–81) as the concentrated meditation on Amitābha Buddha by the recitation of his name; in the Ch'an or Zen tradition, perhaps because the term appears in the Platform Scripture of Hui-neng (cf. Wing-tsit Chan: *The Platform Scripture,* New York, 1963, p. 46), this samadhi has traditionally been regarded as a part of the authentic Zen teaching. It is also called the "samadhi of one aspect (*eka-lakshana samādhi;* Ch., *i-hsiang san-mei*)," perhaps because the term appears in this form in the later version of the *Awakening of Faith* (T32, p. 590c).

53. Said to be the number of heretical doctrines held by non-Buddhist groups in India at the time of Śākyamuni Buddha. There are two traditions: one enumerates ninety-five, the other, ninety-six.

54. No such quotation is found in any of the three basic sutras of the Pure Land School of Buddhism, though the idea expressed is typical of the teachings of that school.

55. The followers of Pure Land Buddhism, having found a confirmation of their beliefs in this celebrated and sophisticated text, have naturally esteemed the *Awakening of Faith* very highly. The fact that this expedient means to salvation for those who are deeply aware of their incapability is given at the end of the section on practice may be considered, in a sense, as indicating the conclusion of the text. Though the faith in Amitābha Buddha is suggested as the seventh item in the Reasons for Writing in the beginning of the text (p. 26), it is somewhat strange that the exhortation to the faith in and meditation on Amitābha Buddha appears immediately after the discussion on the two basic methods of meditation, cessation and clear observation. In fact, this paragraph does not belong to the discussion of the five practices but is an appendix. It is not surprising that one Western scholar, being skeptical of this evidence of Amitābha worship in the text, thought that this paragraph might have been added later by the worshipers of Amitābha or by the author under pressure from a group of Amitābha wor-

shipers. Cf. Walter Liebenthal, "New Light on the Mahāyāna-śraddhotpāda śāstra," *T'oung Pao*, XLVI (1958), 189–97.

56. There has been some feeling among modern scholars that this last section, which is rather crude and propagandizing in tone, is incompatible with the lofty spirit of what has gone before. Some regard it as a later accretion, while some have even taken it as evidence that the entire text was forged in China. As a matter of fact, however, such passages praising the merits of the text are customarily found at the end of the sutras of Mahayana Buddhism, and though the *Awakening of Faith* is not, technically speaking, a sutra, it is not altogether surprising to find such a passage at the conclusion. The section may in fact have been added at a later date by some enthusiastic supporter or supporters of the text, but in the absence of any concrete evidence of that fact it is best to regard it as an integral part of the text.

Selected Bibliography

CLASSICAL COMMENTARIES

Fa-tsang (643–712). *Ta-ch'eng ch'i-hsin lun i-chi*, 5 chŭan. T. No. 1846.

Hui-Yŭan (523–92). *Ta-ch'eng ch'i-hsin lun i-shu*, 4 chŭan. T. No. 1843.

Tzu-hsŭan (d. 1038). *Ch'i-hsin lun shu pi-hsiao-chi*, 20 chŭan. T. No. 1848.

Yuan-hsiao (Wŏnhyo [617–86]). *Ch'i-hsin lun shu*, 2 chŭan. T. No. 1844.

MODERN WORKS

Demiéville, Paul. "Sur l'authenticité du Ta Tch'ing K'i Sin Louen," *Bulletin de la Maison Franco-Japonaise*, II (No. 2, Tokyo, 1929), 1–78.

In this article, the author summarizes the results of study on the problems of the text posed by Japanese scholars up to the date of publication, including a selected bibliography of Japanese publications. For a general background knowledge of the problems, this work is extremely useful.

Hisamatsu Shin'ichi. "Kishin no kadai (The problems of the

awakening of faith)," *Tetsugaku kenkyū* (The journal of philosophical studies) (Kyoto University, 1946), No. 354, pp. 20–45; No. 355, pp. 18–37.

The author discusses the characteristics of the text on the basis of the Reasons for Writing, Part One. The text is analyzed from the point of view of the philosophy of religion.

Itō Kazuo. *Shinchi no tankyū* (The search for true wisdom). Kyoto, 1947. 274 pp.

Three articles collected in this book are strongly recommended for the understanding of the key concepts of the text: "Kishin ni okeru shinnyo no rikai (The understanding of suchness in the awakening of faith)," pp. 25–58; "Shujō no kangensei (Returning to the source of sentient beings)," pp. 59–84; and "Mumyō no kōzō (The structure of ignorance)," pp. 85–106.

Kashiwagi Hiroo. "Shikushananda no yaku to tsutaerareru Daijō kishin ron (On the translation of the awakening of faith in the mahayana attributed to Śikshānanda)," *Journal of Indian and Buddhist Studies*, X (No. 2, March, 1962), 124–25.

The textual differences found between the old and new versions of the *Awakening of Faith* are noted in detail. Though short, this article is useful for textual comparison.

Katō Totsudō. *Daijō kishin ron kōwa* (An explication of the awakening of faith in the mahayana). Tokyo, 1939. 250 pp.

Among the several modern works written in Japanese intended for popularization of the text, this book is recommended. The author interprets the text mainly on the basis of Fa-tsang's commentary.

Liang Ch'i-ch'ao. *Ta-ch'eng ch'i-hsin lun k'ao chêng* (A critical examination of the awakening of faith in the mahayana). Shanghai, 1923. 98 pp.

This book is significant among the works written in Chinese in this period in that it evidences the first critical study of the text applying the historical and philological method of textual criticism. It gives a survey of the results of studies of the text done by Japanese scholars and gives a bibliography of the publications of Japanese scholars on the text (pp. 2–4). The author mainly follows the arguments developed by Mochizuki Shinkō, and claims that the text was neither written by Aśvaghosha nor translated by Paramārtha and that, having been composed in China, it represents an invaluable monument of the synthesis of Chinese and Indian thought. Though the book is included in the *Ta-ch'eng ch'i-hsin lun chên-wei pien,* edited by Shih T'ai-hsü, it is listed separately here because of its historical significance and independent publication.

Liebenthal, Walter. "New Light on the Mahāyāna-śraddhotpāda śāstra," *T'oung Pao,* XLVI (1958), 155–216.

This is a thorough study of the text and its historical problems. The present writer does not agree, in many cases, with the translation of the passages of the text quoted in support of the arguments; nevertheless, this is an important work to be referred to as representing an extremely radical and yet consistent approach to the text.

Mochizuki Shinkō. *Daijō kishin ron no kenkyū* (Studies of the awakening of faith in the mahayana). Kyoto, 1922. 492 pp.

Presented in this book are the author's major articles published earlier in various periodicals, an excellent bibliography on the commentaries and subcommentaries, an analysis of the text, and the old and new versions of the text printed side by side (Appendix, pp. 1–84). This is an indispensable work representing modern critical studies of the text.

Shih T'ai-hsü, ed. *Ta-ch'eng ch'i-hsin lun chên-wei pien* (The authenticity of the awakening of faith in the mahayana). Wu-ch'eng, China, 1924. 102 pp.

This book contains nine articles written by representative Chinese Buddhist scholars of the period. It is valuable in gaining an understanding of how modern Chinese scholars have viewed the problems of the text.

—— *Ta-ch'eng ch'i-hsin lun chiang-i* (Lectures on the awakening of faith in the mahayana). Shanghai, 1921. 2 chüan.

Though written in the present century, this book can be regarded as an extension of the traditional commentary approach. The work gives evidence of the high esteem in which the text is held by the author, the most eminent Chinese Buddhist monk of recent times.

Shih Yin-shun. *Ta-ch'eng ch'i-hsin lun chiang-chi* (Lectures on the awakening of faith in the mahayana). Taipei, 1952. 308 pp.

This is a collection of lectures given on the subject by a

devoted Chinese monk-scholar of today. The language used is more colloquial than literary, and is accordingly easily understandable for a student of modern Chinese. The book may be used as a convenient introduction before one embarks upon the classical commentaries.

Shimaji Daitō. "Daijō kishin ron kaidai" (Introduction to the awakening of faith in the mahayana), *Kokuyaku daizōkyō*, Ronbu, V (Tokyo, 1927), 1–35.

This is an introduction to the author's Japanese translation of the text, giving a comprehensive survey of the textual problems, the studies done on the text in early times, and the influences that the text have exerted upon various schools of Mahayana Buddhism. The summary of the contents of the text given in diagram form is helpful in gaining an over-all picture of the text.

Ui Hakuju. *Daijō kishin ron* (The awakening of faith in the mahayana). (Iwanami edition.) Tokyo, 1936. 148 pp.

This book consists of the critically edited text, a Japanese translation printed on the facing pages, and notes. The notes and the postscript (pp. 131–48) are most useful because of the author's objective approach to the text.

INDEX

Absolute, 13, 15, 28, 31–33; and phenomena, 55–56, synthesis of, 84; absorption into, 115–16n; see also Mind; Suchness

Aeon, 81

Affirmation and negation, 36

Akanishta, 89

Amitābha Buddha, 10–11, 102, 116nn52, 55

Analysis in terms of essence and influence, pattern of, 112n1

Anāsrava, 45

An-āsrava-dharma, 60

An-utpanna, see "Unborn"

Anu-vyañjana (subtle marks) of Sambhogakaya, 70

Arhat(s), 57

A-śūnya-approach, 34

Aśvaghosha, 3, 5–8, 108n6

Attachment(s), 45, 57, 58; to atman, 51; evil, correction of, 73–79

Avalokiteśvara, 62

Avatamsaka (Hua-yen) Sūtra, 49

Avidyā, 46

Awakening of Faith, The: authorship, 3, 5–8; analysis of contents, 3–4, 11–15; commentaries, 4, 9–10; style, 4–5; influence, 10–11, 112n1; terminology, 15–16; translations, 15–18; doubts concerning final section, 117n56

Anxiety, 45

Believers, varieties, 60

Bhikshu Wai-to, see Wai-to

Biased views: of ordinary men, 74–77; of Hinayanists, 78–80

Bliss-body, see Sambhogakaya

Bodhi, see Enlightenment

Bodhisattva(s), 93; early stages of enlightenment, 38; later stages of enlightenment, 39; and understanding of causes of deluded mind, 50; as coordinating causes, 61; and liberation of all men, 63; and Suchness, 63–64; and influence of Suchness as Sambhogakaya, 69–71; realization of Suchness, 71; and vow of universal salvation, 84–85; experience of Dharmakaya, 87–91

Buddha, Triple Body of, 70

Buddha(s), 23, 84; and suffering, 54; as coordinating causes, 61; and liberation of all men, 63; and Suchness, 63–64; and sentient beings, 89–90; faith in, 91; see also Amitābha Buddha; Śākyamuni Buddha

Buddha-Tathāgata(s), 67 ff.

Buddhacarita, 6, 108n6

Cause, primary, 60–61

Causes, coordinating, 60–61

Cessation, 35–36; practice of, 96–100; see also Cessation and clear observation

Cessation and clear observation, practice of, 95

Ch'an (Zen) Buddhism: influenced by Awakening of Faith, 10; non-